The Integrative Mind

The Integrative Mind

*Transformative Education
For a World On Fire*

Tobin Hart

ROWMAN & LITTLEFIELD
Lanham • Boulder • New York • London

Published by Rowman & Littlefield
A wholly owned subsidiary of The Rowman & Littlefield Publishing Group, Inc.
4501 Forbes Boulevard, Suite 200, Lanham, Maryland 20706
www.rowman.com

16 Carlisle Street, London W1D 3BT, United Kingdom

British Library Cataloguing in Publication Information Available

Library of Congress Cataloging-in-Publication Data is available

ISBN 978-1-4758-0700-4 (cloth : alk. paper)
ISBN 978-1-4758-0701-1 (pbk. : alk. paper)
ISBN 978-1-4758-0702-8 (electronic)

♾ ™ The paper used in this publication meets the minimum requirements of American
National Standard for Information Sciences Permanence of Paper for Printed Library
Materials, ANSI/NISO Z39.48-1992.

Printed in the United States of America

For Haley and Maia

Contents

Acknowledgments

Although there are many friends and colleagues who have been influential in shaping these ideas and for whom I am very grateful, I want to reserve special thanks here for just a very few.

I continue to feel gratitude for the support and freedom given from the Department of Psychology at the University of West Georgia, a place where *humanitas* remains front and center. The wisdom and warmth of colleagues and especially students have been instrumental in forming these ideas.

Laura Mae Fenley has been both essential to this project and a joy to work with at every turn. She embodies a one-of-a-kind integrative mind and heart.

My daughters, Maia and Haley, are my constant touchstones and inspiration for considering what matters in life and learning. They have been profound teachers.

My deepest gratitude goes to Mary Mance Hart, whose partnership has been the source of the richest learning and love in my life. She has been central to developing these ideas.

In a few places I have excerpted and modified my words that were previously published in the following books. I wish to thank these publishers: Beyond Words (*The Four Virtues: Presence, Heart, Wisdom, Creation*); New World Library (*The Secret Spiritual World of Children*); Peter Lang (*From Information to Transformation: Education for the Evolution of Consciousness,* 2nd ed.).

Preface

Education is preparation for an uncertain future. The speed and intensity of change—technological, social, and environmental—in this century make this rivetingly clear. From access to instantaneous global communication, to giant buildings collapsing before our eyes, to wind and waves that drown a city, stunning changes seem to define these days and presumably those to come.

But is schooling, with its current emphasis on information acquisition and on basic literacy and numeracy, sufficient to prepare our charges for the realities to come?

It seems clear that there is a gap between my daughters' core curriculum and the core capacities they will need for a life of meaning, value, and success. Banking information and basic skills are necessary but insufficient. Tweaking their curriculum, adjusting standardized testing, and learning on-line have not closed the gap nor seem likely to. Living virtually as live electronic nodes on the information superhighway gives them instant access to nearly anything and everything. But I have become less concerned that they will be able to keep up with the information deluge and more concerned whether they will be able to figure out what is worth keeping up to. How will education for the near horizon help them learn and discern? How will it engender creativity and insight and embody depth and value beyond facts and formulae?

Since we now have access to information with the flick of a finger, what is the point of schooling once we can read, count, and write a bit?

A WORLD ON FIRE

The changes that confront the rising generations are extraordinary. One of the most dramatic recent changes has been the result of microprocessing technology, including its application to communication. Much like the result of the fifteenth century's new information technology, Gutenberg's printing press, computer technology has provided a quantum leap in access and possibility. Kevin Kelly, one of the founders of *Wired* magazine, describes this remarkable new reality as he imagines what a review of these days at the edge of the third millennium will look like from three thousand years into the future:

> Humans began animating inert objects with tiny slivers of intelligence, connecting them into a global field, and linking their own minds into a single thing. This will be recognized as the largest, most complex, and most surprising event on the planet. Weaving nerves out of glass and radio waves, our species began wiring up all regions, all processes, and facts, all notions into a grand network. From this embryonic neural net was born a collaborative interface for our civilization. [1]

Who knows whether historians in the future will see it in the same way, but he makes the point that when we step back for a moment we can recognize that the change we are in the midst of is pretty astounding.

Alongside the unprecedented potential inherent in this information age, we also find ourselves deluged with surround-sound violence and sexuality, sucked downstream by materialism and marketing, pushed along with hurried schedules and instant communication. How do we see what is of value in this sea of information?

The effect is not just on our brand loyalty or texting habits. The influence goes all the way down from the global network to our social network to our neural net. Technology is shaping our minds. We are becoming functioning hybrids: part human, part machine turned on and linked up. Technology already provides powerful augmentations to our minds allowing us to: outsource memory; open new possibilities for "public thinking" as we discover that a blog post can bring responses from around the world; gain near instant access to news and to nonsense; calculate—what computers do best—faster than the human mind can do (IBM's Watson supercomputer can parse two hundred million pages of information in three seconds), [2] giving us opportunities to see, for example, statistical patterns in "big data."

Of course not all the changes to mind may be what we hope for. Will clicking our way through fragments of information reduce our ability for sustained concentration and depth of comprehension? Will so much time on disembodied screens reduce our connections to our own bodies, the body of nature, and direct, embodied encounters with one another? Invisible algorithmic editing is customizing the information that comes to us by way of the Internet through engines like Google. This tends to give us patterns of information that are similar to information we have already viewed—more of the same—thereby reducing exposure to diverse content and different points of view; will these invisible algorithms reduce our capacity to see broadly and choose wisely? There is evidence and argument that for all the advantages of massive computational power, these not-so-desirable changes are already shaping us.[3]

There are plenty of other changes afoot today. A quickly changing, indeterminate future filled with global competition and political uncertainties means that the marketplace may not look to our children like the one we know or our parents knew. The First World is no longer providing life-long jobs and guaranteed pensions. A graduating student from high school or college may have more than a dozen different jobs in their future, if they are lucky enough to find work. Degree inflation means we spend more time in school to get to the previous threshold of employment but without any guarantees of work. Will graduates have the dexterity of mind and skill to adapt?

These days are also intense. Stress is implicated in the top causes of death in the industrialized world.[4] Global climate, economic, environmental, and political change wreak all sorts of havoc and require new adaptations. Global population has just topped seven billion; just thirty years ago we were at three billion.[5] The gap between the haves and the have-nots grows wider; the list of changes goes on and on, and change becomes the new norm.

The military has an acronym for this intensity, "VUCA," which stands for volatility, uncertainty, complexity, and ambiguity. In the face of this intensity it may be hard to avoid becoming dizzy or numb, drugged or distracted, angry or quietly desperate. Suicide and homicide are the second and third leading causes of teen deaths, respectively. According to the National Institute of Mental Health, half of the adult population will have a diagnosable mental disorder over the course of their lifetime. Half. In any given year, one quarter of the U.S. population is diagnosable with one or more psychiatric disorders. Thirty-five million Americans have severe depression; fifty-six million have an anxiety disorder. It is predicted that by 2020 depression will be the second most common health problem in the world.[6] How will young people develop the capacities to find balance in their lives?

This is a world on fire with possibility and with peril. Is it reasonable to think that education can prepare us for these demands? If education is to prepare us for the future, how can it not?

VACUUM OR VISION?

Recent approaches to change in education have emphasized assessment, curricular standards, and technology.

Considerable effort over more than a decade has focused on standardized assessment. Universal, summative assessment can give us some useful data, but, as the evidence increasingly demonstrates, this has not given us better schools, teachers, students, or society or even meaningfully better test scores. This leveraging of test scores has been like the tail wagging the dog and has proved inadequate for significant and meaningful improvement. We need to hold a bigger view of education than this.

Emphasis on core standards (some 1,500 discrete skills in the current U.S. national initiative) gives specific targets for schooling. The problem is not with reasonable standards themselves; the problem is when they become the new bits and bytes commodified, prepped for, tested, and checked off a list. If they follow the current trend, they will too often remain out of context and out of contact.

Massive open online courses (MOOCs) or something similar provides access to organized information and degrees at a lower price point. This is helpful for many who have lacked opportunity around the world. But this does not touch the fundamental problems of contemporary education. In fact, it will entrench those problems further as an outmoded educational motif becomes more "efficiently" delivered to more individuals. In a sense it extends the inadequacies of an old operating system of contemporary education more efficiently: more modernist assumptions pumped through an information-age delivery system. It risks becoming even more about degrees without addressing depth, information without integration, a cheaper means to an unimproved and likely diluted end.

In general, throwing the responsibility of "saving education" to technology places a valuable tool in a role it cannot fulfill. Of course a world-class lecture or more individually paced lessons or easy access to information and peer responses can be tremendously valuable. But in the end, new technology is neither education's demise nor its salvation. It provides another tool, especially powerful to be sure, that we can shape and that shapes us.

Defining the problem as college or high school graduation rates, student loan debt, standardized test scores, the need for more online learning, comparison of postgraduation income rates, or whatever metric comes along will not touch the more fundamental questions of educational quality and relevance. These data may reflect problems or business opportunities, but if we spend our energy solving the wrong problem we will miss the forest for the trees. We will see shortly the out-of-date assumptions that underpin and doom approaches built around these metrics.

Despite the enormous financial, intellectual, and even spiritual wealth that the First World possesses, for the most part we seem helpless to actually improve public education significantly. It has been like moving a mountain with a spoon. Thirty years after the famous U.S. National Commission on Excellence in Education report entitled *A Nation at Risk*, we are a nation and a world at greater risk. As that report concluded: "If an unfriendly power had attempted to impose on America the mediocre educational performance that exists today, we might well have viewed it as an act of war. As it stands, we have allowed this to happen to ourselves."[7] Thirty years down the road are we better off? Thirty years from now, will we be?

Part of the current obstacle toward sustained and substantial change in education is a "technical" problem: we are using an outmoded operating system. Much of contemporary education is guided by a nineteenth-century, industrial-age model of learning not well suited for this information age. We do not have an educational vision that is adequate for the second half of the twentieth century, much less for the twenty-first. Instead we are left in a kind of vacuum. Without an upgraded vision we will be distracted from essential change by the next initiative on classroom management, new scheduling formats, online learning, standards, technology as panacea, or whatever the next thing turns out to be.

The history of education is strewn with well-intentioned initiatives that either did not stick or became diluted and distorted from their original intent. Long-term teachers are accustomed to the next innovative program; it has as long a shelf life as perhaps an assistant principal: viable, sort of, until the next good idea comes along or the political or economic winds change. Piecemeal or new programs, however noble, are difficult to sustain within the current system.

At the most fundamental level, education is about two overarching and interrelated goals: serving society and developing the potential of the individual. Public education was explicitly founded to train workers for the marketplace, an industrial marketplace of the nineteenth century. This was a reasonable but incomplete goal that continues to drive much of our educational policy, even though the actual results are often out of step for a nonhomogenous and postindustrial society. For example, the recent IBM face-to-face study of more than 1,700 CEOs across the globe identifies four traits that are most associated with employees' future success: collaboration, communication, creativity, and flexibility. Outperforming organizations themselves are especially characterized by openness rather than rigid controls, a culture of cocreated and shared values, and ability and willingness to embrace change.[8] These are not the emphases that leap to mind when we think of our contemporary educational system.

A balanced approach understands that the well-being of the individual is essential for the health of a society and, reciprocally, a healthy society invites the flowering of diverse human potential. I think we can find some real agreement around these two core values about what education needs to be about for the twenty-first century.

While much educational aspiration and rhetoric probably already falls in line with these notions, the reality is that it is hard to say that we are preparing for either the good of the individual or of society, much less both.

Today, if education is about information and if information now lives in a device in our pocket, what is education for? The simplistic emphasis built around basic information acquisition truncated and instantiated through over-emphasis on test scores misses a genuine consideration of depth and has distracted us from the big questions. What kind of person and populous do we want and need for the world of today and tomorrow? Values should determine structures, not the other way around. Instead of emphasizing assessment, curricular adjustments, and online delivery, I want to reconsider the vision that we hold for education in this dynamic age, the pedagogy that can help us achieve it, and the human consciousness that underlies it all. Most fundamentally, the question I wonder about is this: What kind of mind do we need for today and tomorrow and how can schooling foster it?

NOTES

1. Kevin Kelly, "We Are the Web," *Wired* 13, no. 8, August 2005, 205.

2. Clive Thompson, *Smarter Than You Think: How Technology Is Changing Our Minds for the Better* (New York: Penguin Press, 2013), 282.

3. Nicholas Carr, *The Shallows: What the Internet Is Doing to Our Brains* (New York: W. W. Norton, 2011).

4. "Leading Causes of Death," Centers for Disease Control and Prevention, www.cdc.gov/nchs/fastats/lcod.htm. The influence of stress on these causes of death (heart disease, cancer, chronic lower respiratory disease, and stroke) has been widely recognized. For an excellent overview of mind-body interaction, see Henry Dreher, *Mind-Body Unity: A New Vision for Mind-Body Science and Medicine* (Baltimore: Johns Hopkins University Press, 2003).

5. "US and World Population Clock," U.S. Census Bureau, accessed August 2013, www.census.gov/popclock.

6. R. C. Kessler, P. A. Berglund, O. Demler, R. Jin, and E. E. Walters, "Lifetime Prevalence and Age-of-Onset Distributions of DSM-IV Disorders in the National Comorbidity Survey Replication (NCS-R)," *Archives of General Psychiatry* 62, no. 6 (2005): 593–602.

7. "A Nation at Risk: The Imperative for Educational Reform," *National Commission on Excellence in Education*, April 1983, 5.

8. "Leading Through Connections: Insights from the Global Chief Executive Officer Study," IBM Corporation, May 2012.

Introduction

What kind of mind do we need for the days to come? How can education best serve society and the individual? What is the horizon of consciousness, culture, and classrooms?

There is a place where developing the mind, growing the potential of the individual, and serving society was the central mission of education: the original liberal arts. The liberal arts have a 2,500-year history originating from the ancient Greeks. This was the original schooling for the free man and the means to preserve such freedom. These were disciplines to help one develop the mind through reflection, study, and practice.

These original seven arts were divided into two categories that should seem familiar: the trivium, consisting of the verbal arts of logic, grammar, and rhetoric; and the quadrivium, consisting of the numerical arts of mathematics, geometry, music, and astronomy. This looks a lot like today's SATs with a melody. The language arts were taught earliest, as they were essential for everything that followed. Mathematics blended in soon thereafter. We do the same thing 2,500 years later.

This ancient approach is the very literal foundation for formal education in the West. But the central organizing principles and practices of the liberal arts are something we might not always recognize in today's version. It was not exactly content that was the key, although information was and must remain the *currency* of learning.

Liberal, as in liberal arts, is often understood to mean broad, as in broadly educated: some of this and some of that. But the root of the word *liberal* is the same as for *liberty* and *liberation*; it is about freedom, not merely knowing lots of different stuff. These were the arts of liberty. The goal was freedom from ignorance, from prejudice, and from out-of-control "passions" such as lust and greed. The learning was about cultivating the freedom to choose wisely, to develop reason, grow in virtue, to create our work and our life in a way that serves and satisfies. This was the meaning of the *The Good Life.*

The ultimate function of the liberal arts was to secure the liberation of the mind. The integrative principle is *humanitas.* The fullness of our humanity is revealed and may flourish through this inner growth. Our human potential for the good of self and society was to be liberated in this way. Historian Pierre Hadot described the high end of these original liberal arts as "a method for training people to live and look at the world in a new way. It is an attempt to transform human kind."[1] The roots of our education are about preparing us for a life of flourishing and fulfillment by developing our humanity, our human consciousness, our mind and soul.

The Renaissance found some of its inspiration through the rediscovery of ancient Greek ideas. This period profoundly opened human horizons in ways that we still celebrate, even revere. For example, the likes of da Vinci and Michelangelo are twenty-first-century icons representing qualities of genius. However, the visions and values that are often associated with the ancient Greek and early Renaissance eras have undergone significant changes that have been shaping our consciousness and culture ever since.

Philosopher Stephen Toulmin argues that from the sixteenth to the seventeenth centuries there was a particular turning away of earlier Renaissance values. The intellectual fashion became more rigid and dogmatic and reason itself became narrower, no longer respecting context or appreciating diversity to the same degree.[2]

Four hundred years ago Sir Francis Bacon helped to steer that turn with the articulation of inductive reasoning and of what we come to recognize as the scientific method. He understood just what this implied for education: "Mastery of nature for the relief of man's estate begins to become the governing objective of education." The aim was no longer to teach people how to live well or to develop their humanity; it was to "enlarge the power and empire of mankind in general over the universe."[3] It looks like we have succeeded remarkably well in expanding our powers over the universe. In Rene Descartes' words, "[We have rendered] ourselves the lords and possessors of nature."[4] But in gaining that power we risk losing something else.

ABBREVIATORS

This shift in knowing that both Bacon and Descartes were so instrumental in establishing has helped us to distinguish, dissect, define, and develop in so many domains. This has been incredible by any measure. One of the cornerstones has been differentiation. We see differentiation now embodied in the separation of educational disciplines, of facts from context, the specialization of and within professions such as medicine, and the emphasis on measurement such as testing of bits of information in education.

This individual, detached perspective is hinged on a way of knowing that separates it (the object of study) from us—objectification—and often by reducing it to constituent parts—reductionism. Objectification and reductionism (alongside assumptions of materialism, dualism, mechanism, and determinism) are the primary tools of the modernist way of knowing and tend to engender knowing by a kind of domination, as Bacon and Descartes implied. In a sense the "other" is to be known by detachment from it and our dominion over it. Whether the atom or our neighboring state or a competing ideology, we might say the work is to tame it to our will.

As powerful and valuable as this is—and there is absolutely no denying its worth—we are recognizing the limits and unintended consequences of this way of knowing. It tends to leave us and the world fragmented, out of context, and out of balance.

Perhaps no one articulated the limits of this way of knowing better than someone who lived a century before Bacon and Descartes. Leonardo da Vinci understood the problem of what he called the *abbreviators* approach. His words seem startlingly prophetic now five hundred years later:

> The abbreviators of works do injury to knowledge and to love. . . . Of what value is he who, in order to abbreviate the parts of those things of which he professes to give complete knowledge, leaves out the greater part of the things of which the whole is composed? . . . You don't see that you are falling into the same error as one who strips the tree of its adornment of branches full of leaves, intermingled with fragrant flowers or fruit, in order to demonstrate that the tree is good for making planks.[5]

Da Vinci's approach was an integrated science, philosophy, and art of quality and wholeness, an exploration of patterns, systems, and the interrelatedness of things, more complete than the mechanistic and reductionistic understanding.[6] He understood the parts and the mechanics; he designed hundreds of mechanical devices and carefully studied their properties, including precise understanding of things like the human arm or of the flow of fluids—hydraulics—recognizing its applicability to everything from water in a stream to blood flow in the body.

But while he understood full well that the arm, for example, provided mechanical utility and could be dissected into individual components, he did not reduce the arm or the human or nature at large simply to mechanics. His reverence for natural creations and his ability to recognize patterns and interconnecting phenomena provided an integrated science and art, value and meaning, rationality and beauty. Without this larger, more integrated way of knowing, as he says, we "do injury to knowledge and to love."

To what extent does our prevailing educational approach leave out parts of the mind—ways of knowing—and thereby foster the same kind of injury? Today, how do we reconcile mechanistic and holistic understanding, awe and information, quality and quantity, and while we are at it, find what the ancient Greeks searched for—the good, the true, and the beautiful?

THE FRONTIER OF CULTURE AND CONSCIOUSNESS

Confusion arises in education today particularly because we are in the midst of an epochal change and we cannot quite clearly make out the horizon and thus how education should best proceed. Civilization appears to move through various eras or epochs of knowing, that is, the grounds on which we constitute truth and knowledge. Philosopher Michel Foucault referred to this as the *episteme* of an era.[7] Thomas Kuhn spoke of scientific *paradigms* in a fairly similar although more circumscribed way.[8] Basically, the episteme is made up of the assumptions, rules, roles, standards, and methods of knowing that guide and limit how we think and know. We cannot quite see this; it is a kind of epistemic unconscious or underlying field that we operate within. This matrix forms the conditions and limits of possibility for knowledge in a given time and place. Such an epoch of knowing emerges from, overlaps with, and then eclipses the previous episteme. For example, we might conclude that the early Renaissance was followed by a modernist period. (Because culture is not homogenous, multiple epistemes could coexist as part of different power-knowledge systems or subcultures.) We can recognize some of the characteristics of the predominant modernist episteme of the past few centuries including the role of the individual, the application of a scientistic, materialist, reductionist, objectivist knowing as the standard for truth. This naturally led to education that emphasizes facts, measurement, control, predictability, generality, reduction, materiality, and the like. It also would tend to miss observations and conclusions that land outside that episteme.

More recently, the postmodern turn has opened great cracks in the modernist episteme. It helps us unpack facts and ask critical questions about knowledge. For example, we recognize that truth and knowledge are often tied to power. When we ask, "Who funded that research?" we are recognizing the mutability of objective fact. Truth is mediated by our intent, expectations, social status, language, race, history, and more. In Washington and elsewhere we may now even refer to "true facts" revealing this postmodern recognition of just how facts can be a product of power and spin, not only reduced, objective, certain, and measureable.

I want to make clear that this in no way whatsoever diminishes the importance of science or facts or measurement or logic, but it places them in the context of human understanding and culture. It helps us think critically and go behind the curtain of so-called objective knowledge. We can thank this postmodern shift for elevating critical reasoning and questioning, helping us recognize that "truth," to one degree or another, is socially construed.

The modernist era has helped us to distinguish in so many ways. The postmodern has helped expose how culture and context shape what we consider to be true and good and beautiful. But we are on the cusp of something more.

The challenge for this new era is not just to differentiate, dominate, or deconstruct, but instead to *integrate*. An industrial era yields to the information age, but the front edge is not merely about more information, it is instead an age of integration. Goethe said it this way: "To locate yourself in the infinite you must distinguish and then unite."[9]

We already see the harbingers of a drive toward integration in all sorts of front-edge initiatives: mind-body medicine; the fusion of art, music, and technology; East-West dialogue in everything from culture to cuisine; neurophenomenology as a research approach to merge direct experience and brain activity; social neuroscience that challenges the assumptions of discrete, individual consciousness, recognizing the linking of brains; new previously inconceivable blended fields like neuroaesthetics and neuroethics; lessons from paleobiology being applied to global finance;[10] tide pool ecology informing approaches to post–9/11 national security;[11] and the largest annual academic prize being the Templeton Prize for the integration of science and spirituality, two domains that have been radically segregated for four hundred years. We are coming to recognize interconnection in everything from pollution to politics to persons.

The fundamental assumptions of reality that underlie the modernist episteme are not only being deconstructed but also being turned upside down. We are moving from an understanding of the world as chunks of dead matter to seeing it as part of a self-organizing, living universe. In domain after domain we are coming to recognize connection, interdependence, and integration at every level of being. With it we have the possibility and the need, in the words of Thomas Berry, to move from seeing the world as a collection of objects to experiencing it as a communion of subjects.[12]

However partial our view of the horizon is, we are standing in a position that enables us to recognize many of the features of this knowing: integrating versus abbreviating, holistic versus reductionistic, connection versus domination, emergent and coconstituted versus materially existent and individual, value-laden versus valueless, interdependent versus isolated, dynamic versus static, probabilistic rather than deterministic, subjective and objective, intuition and logic, forest and tree, commonality and difference, compassion and calculation.

The challenge for this age is not just about more information and faster connections, more differentiation and domination, but to find a way to bring together the bits and the bytes in living the integrated life in a world of global interconnection so that we, as da Vinci warned, stop doing injury to knowledge and to love. If our education and our consciousness are to be a match for this century, this is where the trail of knowing leads. But how do we proceed?

TWO WAYS OF KNOWING

Our understanding of knowing is multifaceted and in education emphasizes memory, reasoning, learning style, language, intelligence, and on and on. Acknowledging the vast array of distinctions, I want to cut beneath these to claim that with respect to education, consciousness, and culture today, there are two ways of knowing. That is, there are two fundamental ways that the mind works to know the world. There are myriad variations to be sure and certainly plenty of other ways to slice this rhetorically, but the most salient concern today comes down to this.

One way we will call *categorical*. This knows the world through abstraction, through separating it from us, through taking apart to understand. In a sense everything is reduced to parts, to lowest units that are differentiated, named, catalogued. It reaches its apex in metaphor of computer zeroes and ones. Categorical awareness narrows in to focus on detail and seeks precision, objectivity, and presupposes certainty. It simplifies and represents, proceeds linearly and sequentially, and generalizes. Our schooling emphasizes this way of knowing, and for the most part, only this.

The other knowing is through *contact* instead of category. Its style is direct, relational, embodied, and recognizes wholes and connections. Awareness through contact enables a broader view, one connected with the world and the body, scanning for changes in the environment. This knowing seeks novelty, picks up implicit meaning and metaphor, is able to read faces and other cues of individuals instead of simplified, predetermined, and generalized categories. Knowledge through contact is evolving, implicit, and indeterminate since it always exists in relationship to something else and is not ever fully graspable.

Iain McGilchrist, drawing from a vast body of neuroscientific and phenomenological data, makes a compelling case that these ways of knowing have neurological substrates corresponding to the anatomically distinct hemispheres of the brain.[13] Though there was some popular interest in right-left hemisphere distinction at the later part of the twentieth century, the common understanding was largely inaccurate, often reducing the left to basic logic and the right to creativity. Logic and creativity and most other complex functions involve interaction across brain and body regions.

However, today we are recognizing that left and right hemispheres of the brain, generally speaking, do *process* differently. They are involved with two fundamentally different ways of relating to the world. The left largely enables that categorical, narrowed, discriminative focus while the attention of the right is broad and flexible, able to recognize connected wholes as opposed to the left's individual parts. These seem perfectly designed to complement one another, and both ways of knowing are essential to human understanding. The problem is that their essential partnership has come unhinged.

One of McGilchrist's primary insights is that categorical consciousness does not have the capacity to integrate the more contact-full way of knowing. By its very nature it cannot process or value in wholes or draw material from the body and senses so readily (most sensory and body-based information connects neurologically to the brain through the right hemisphere). On the other hand, the right is largely integrative and naturally incorporates the data from the left and is thus positioned to serve as the dominant driver of consciousness.

Because of the powerful rise of categorical consciousness reinforced through objectivism and reductionism and the education that both derives from and reinforces it, the consciousness associated with the right has lost its primacy; the left is running the show. Inevitably, the show it can see is limited, an abstracted or virtual view of the world but one assumed to be real and more or less complete. The result is what da Vinci would call an abridged or abbreviated approach with its powerful implications for what we recognize (knowledge) and how we behave (love).

There are other accounts of the dual nature of mind that fall roughly along the same lines. For example, we hear reference to masculine and feminine aspects of knowing and being. In Chinese philosophy, two distinct ways of being are represented as the familiar yin and yang, dependent and embedded in one another. In ancient yogic theory two channels of energy—Ida and Pingala—spiral up the spine. The ancient Greek caduceus—two serpents coiling around a staff—gives an image to help picture this, as does the spiral of DNA. Ida represents the feminine, intuitive energies, said to tie to the brain's right hemisphere. Pingala represents the masculine or rational consciousness and connects to the left hemisphere. The story goes that when these are in balance, a third and the greatest channel of energy—the Sushumna—is activated, enabling a great rising of consciousness. There is not space here to elaborate but only to make the point that these general distinctions are recognized as fundamental aspects of consciousness across traditions and times.

Ultimately the most important consideration is not what these functions are called or where they are identified anatomically. Given the complexity of consciousness, our understanding will continue to unfold. The essential significance is in recognizing the distinct *capacities* of mind, the ways that we attend to the world and just how that shapes what we see.

Education, along with most attempts to improve it, is embedded in an operating system that validates one aspect of knowing but only dimly recognizes there is something to the other side. This other knowing moves us, gives us context, it may even transform us, but we cannot measure or manipulate or manage it in the same way and thus it has been devalued.

The front edge of consciousness and culture involves rebalancing these ways of knowing. We have focused on the function that takes things apart, that meets the world at arm's length, that works off categories and abstractions, and assumes certainty. We also want and need to meet it up close and in person, to feel it in our bodies, to recognize wholes and not only parts, to feel awe and mystery, to be moved, find context, meaning, and beauty, so that the bits and bytes make sense. We do not need to just catalogue our life; we need to enter it.

How do we integrate the powerful precision of categorical consciousness with the big view and intimate touch of contact? How do we improve our ability to not only generate consciousness but also to receive it? Is it even possible or practical to go about this in our daily life and in contemporary education? There is no switch to flip or control knob to turn.

Maybe this sounds too much to hope for or maybe too ephemeral for the classroom or the marketplace, or maybe you simply are not buying the value of this shift in knowing or even that consciousness operates in these ways. But I will try to show not only how essential this is but also how immediately and easily available this opening and balancing of mind is without radical change in standards or curriculum. It requires reconsideration of human consciousness—of how we know—and with it, how education can best proceed.

KNOWER, KNOWING, KNOWLEDGE

Knowledge comes always and only through us. That is, *how* we know, and *who* we are, affects *what* we know. Anaïs Nin made the point this way, "We don't see things as they are. We see things as we are."[14] For education, the most fundamental level of integration is between *knowledge, knower,* and *knowing.* To move beyond the current educational impasse, a recalibration of these three is required. This places an emphasis not only on what we are to know—knowledge, which has been the primary emphasis of schooling—but more explicitly on knower and knowing—the inner life and processes that make us go and know.

In learning, we already know that moving knower and knowledge closer to one another makes a difference. For example, science and technical education benefit from hands-on wherever possible, history from context and story, every subject from relevance and immediacy because they activate emotions and move the subject matter nearer to us and us to it. When we meet and speak with the stranger or live in her shoes for a bit, we invariably gain new understanding for her world. When we go into the field in some way we have a better chance of recognizing systems, interconnections, ecologies, and economies; when we can touch it and take it in, we are more likely to embody the learning; when we can enter and reflect on our own inner experience we can be transformed by it.

In a very real sense we have left knower and knowing behind in favor of a narrow bandwidth of knowledge, abbreviated, downloaded, and assessed. We have recognized that this has left out much of what we hope education would do for society and the self, and so we have tried to add "soft" approaches to bridge to the person, to try to touch our humanity in some way or at least make students ready for polite company. California schools thought that self-esteem was a key and mandated programs in schools to cheer on the student's self-worth. Character education and similar initiatives have tried to address considerations of civility. Important initiatives in social and emotional learning and on contemplative teaching and learning emphasize that the inner and interpersonal are essential to well-being.

The problem is not with these well-intended directions. In many cases they are filling a need and making a difference. The issue is in recognizing that the system in which they are operating is outdated. The vision and view of education and of human consciousness are simply not adequate for this century, and so these programs remain add-ons to the "serious" curriculum and thus are likely to be unsustainable. When the political, economic, administrative, or social winds change, these programs may become distorted or diluted or fall by the wayside altogether. A more fundamental and integrated solution is possible, one that goes to the very heart of learning, to human consciousness and to the root of the difficulty, emphasizing *how* we know.

Integrating knower and knowing as well as knowledge changes the fundamental operating principles. The emphasis is not against traditional literacy, numeracy, and vocational skills or against technology or professionalism or even improved test scores; instead it brings *depth* to it all.

Recalibrating knower, knowing, and knowledge in teaching and learning gives us a better shot at growing minds, not just loading them up. Consciousness stands on content but is not reduced to it. An integrated approach returns information and basic skills to their rightful place as currency of education and returns the mind (knower and knowing) as the primary agent and target for teaching.

MISSING MINDS

The mind that the ancients sought to develop, that great minds like da Vinci seemed to embody, and that is required to move human consciousness and culture forward is a mind that imagines new possibilities and draws across what we now consider separate subjects; it is creative and flexible, seeks novelty, yet is capable of precision. This is also a mind that seeks and sees beauty, cultivates values, engages in self-reflection, creative expression, and a search for meaning and purpose, and each is unique. The high end of this consciousness is not merely pluralistic; it is integrative.

With respect to education we still gather around the fire of information, and reading, writing, and reasoning remain the focus of learning, but now mind is at the head of the class, transforming both self and subject. A change of mind is, of course, what we hope and assume schools have been doing all along—the great idea or the new skill changes us. But for some time schooling has been thinking about thinking in an abbreviated way, too often an almost mechanical process that reduces knowledge to factoids, replaces problem solving with answer giving, and narrows the bandwidth of intellect.

Without attention to the fullness of mind we may sense, especially as children, that something is missing. At some level we know we are not getting the whole story; it does not seem quite right, not as juicy as we thought the life of learning would be and thus not as nourishing and sustaining in and of itself. Intrinsic motivation wanes, a subtle resistance can take root, and potentials lie undeveloped. We presume that the massive emphasis on information and basic skills—reading, writing, and numeracy—would at least lead to a populous that could do those things well. But we know this is not the case for so many. We need the balance of mind in order for these activities to have context, meaning, and immediacy and be embodied within us. The seduction of information, the objectification of knowing, the anxiety of accountancy, and the detachment of the knower have left us too often holding the shell and leaving the nut behind. We need more mind than that.

In what follows, five gateways into more integrative and balanced knowing are elaborated. We could even think of these as the recovery of missing minds.

Contemplative Mind

Perhaps the most fundamental injunction for learning is to pay attention. Yet we rarely help children to do this, we just insist that they do. To deploy, shift, sustain, and open awareness gives us power to use the mind intentionally. The most basic and universal practices of contemplation do just this, developing the strength and flexibility of the muscle of attention. In addition, the contemplative mind allows us to do more. With just a little practice we can turn our gaze inward, witness the content and the process of our own consciousness, helping to clean and even reground the lens of perception in order to see the world, including ourselves, more clearly.

This reflection leads to metacognition, which allows us to inquire not only into the question at hand but also toward the asker of the question. We can become the object of inquiry as well as the instrument, as we inquire into self and subject. Ultimately, contemplative mind allows us to interrupt habitual patterns and reactions and stay awake to new ways of thinking and seeing, to the flow of consciousness inside and out.

In addition, the attention to attention has a variety of related effects. This inner technology allows us to steady the mind and modulate emotional reaction, reduce stress response in the body, and foster executive function especially important at a time when the outer world is pushing so much, so fast at us. A contemplative way of knowing has the potential to alter the function and even the structure of the brain and with it shift long-term traits such as compassion and emotional balance.

Empathic Mind

While science, or more precisely, scientism, claims a detached, objective gaze at objects, the way great scientists do science is often quite different from the way we teach it. Specifically there is a less detached empiricism at work where the gap between knower and the object of study is reduced. Nobel laureate in genetics Barbara McClintock says it this way: "You have to have a feeling for the organism; you have to have an openness to let it come to you."[15] Not only in science but in all domains, a capacity to put one's self in another's shoes provides a multiplicity of perspectives, helping us understand how a terrorist might, from another point of view, be a freedom fighter or vice versa. This allows us to reconsider our own assumptions as well as the other's vantage point.

As we close the distance between self and object something else happens. We become less willing to do violence to the other, whether a tree or our neighbor. In fact, empathy has been described as the trait that makes us most human and the foundation for morality. Thus, a more intimate empiricism has profound implications for values and virtue, caring and civility, domains that education has been tasked to develop. When we open to this level of understanding we find the mind most often naturally includes the heart.

Empathy is about a way of meeting the world. It opens the possibility for collaboration, community, and communion and with it a more intimate sense of interconnection and interdependence, so essential for a global society.

Beautiful Mind

The ancients knew that somehow the goal of life was not only about the good and the true; it was also beautiful. In his novel *The Idiot*, Dostoevsky says, "Beauty will save the world."[16] Philosopher Alfred North Whitehead says the "teleology of the universe is the production of beauty."[17] Somehow beauty embodies something both immanent and transcendent that resonates deep within us. We recognize it, we seek it, we base decisions on it; we might call it "quality." Even in science we discover beauty may be the prime mover. French mathematician and theoretical physicist Henri Poincaré understood the role of beauty in science in this way:

> The scientist does not study nature because it is useful to do so. He studies it because he takes pleasure in it; and he takes pleasure in it because it is beautiful.[18]

One of the primary sources of beauty is nature: a spectacular sunset, the redness of a rose, the majesty of the flight of a hawk. Nature serves as wonder for the mind. The beautiful mind—that is, attention to beauty, quality, or an aesthetic—is not ancillary but instead central to an integrative mind.

Embodied Mind

Despite our sometime obsession with the body, especially some bodies, we have underestimated its role in knowing. From Augustine to Descartes the body has been understood as primitive and mechanistic. But contemporary neuroscience and our lived experience begins to paint a picture of a body—feeling, sensation, movement, physiological processes—that is not separate or inferior to thinking but instead central and integrated with knowing. From this new understanding, education is dramatically catalyzed by attention to the body, developing an embodied mind we might say. The mind-body unity helps put our parts back together and with it comes a return of a more robust way of knowing cultivated by attunement to the body.

In addition to becoming more attuned to the body, embodiment means integrating the abstract and the concrete, idea and action through hands-on activity and in the context of our daily life. In Waldorf education we learn to cook, in shop we learn how to take an engine apart by actually taking an engine apart. A feedback loop is created and thus a powerful means for learning when we take action in the world. Our powers of observation, of refined discrimination, self-discipline, deduction and calculation, systematic experimentation, and problem solving all are activated when we embody an idea in an action.

Imaginative Mind

In general, there has been a tendency in the modern West not to take imagination seriously. The nonobservable, nonlogical nature of imagination renders it difficult to pin down and thus awkward in a rationalist, materialist backdrop. Imagination has been mistaken as merely a colorful accent to life and largely dismissed in an educational age anxious about meeting standards and status. However, we do not outgrow imagination individually or culturally, as this process is fundamental to our knowing at every level of development and across every significant domain. We hear, for example, that imagination is the source of insight from scientific discovery to artistic innovation to practical problem solving. The activities of mind that produced the inventions of da Vinci, the sonnets of Shakespeare, and declarations of liberty are not adequately explained through sequential logic and amassing of facts. Improvisation, divergent thinking, play, fantasy, myth, spontaneity, irony, metaphor, and design are at home here as we imagine possibility beyond the information given, so essential in this dynamic age.

At this moment education is developmentally stuck. We seem unable to meaningfully improve our current educational outcomes, and we may not be able to go any further as a society with the educational emphasis that we have. Sure, some of us will benefit and get ahead, some of us will get rich and get good test scores, but it is hard to say what our minds and our society are developing into through this educational route. Are we growing our humanity or something else? Currently education leaves out critical aspects of mind. Da Vinci would conclude that we have taken an abbreviator's approach and with it lost our minds or at least our way. In an age that is on fire with so much possibility and so much peril, our satisfaction and perhaps our very survival require all the mind that we can get.

Ultimately, emphasis on an integrative mind invites the most ancient and enduring aspirations for education and human flourishing: liberation of each mind to seek and create the good, the true, and the beautiful.

NOTES

1. Pierre Hadot, *Philosophy as a Way of Life: Spiritual Exercises from Socrates to Foucault*, ed. Arnold Davidson (Oxford: Blackwell Publishing, 1995), 107.

2. Stephen Toulmin, *Cosmopolis: The Hidden Agenda of Modernity* (Chicago: University of Chicago Press, 1992).

3. Francis Bacon, "Novum Organum," in *Advancement of Learning and Novum Organum* (New York: Wiley Book Co.,1900), 315, 366.

4. Rene Descartes, *A Discourse on Method: Meditations and Principles* (New York: J. M. Dent, 1994), 45; original work published 1637.

5. As cited in Frijof Capra, *The Science of Leonardo* (New York: Doubleday, 2007), 12.

For another translation, see Leonardo da Vinci, "Against Writers of Epitomes," *The Literary Works of Leonardo da Vinci*, vol. II, trans. and ed. Jean Paul Richter (London: Sampson Low, Marston, Searle & Rivington, 1883), 302.

6. Ibid.

7. Michel Foucault, *The Archeology of Knowledge,* trans. A. M. Sheridan Smith (New York: Routledge, 2002); original work published 1969.

8. Thomas S. Kuhn, *The Structure of Scientific Revolutions* (Chicago: University of Chicago Press, 1962).

9. Johann Wolfgang von Goethe, excerpt from *Atmosphäre*, in Paul Bishop, *Analytical Psychology and German Classical Aesthetics: Goethe, Schiller, and Jung,* vol. 1 (New York: Routledge, 2008), 48.

10. R. M. May, S. A. Levin, G. Sugihara, "Ecology for Bankers," *Nature* 451 (2008): 893–895.

11. Rafe Sagarin, *Learning from the Octopus: How Secrets from Nature Can Help Us Fight Terrorist Attacks, Natural Disasters, and Disease* (New York: Basic Books, 2012).

12. Thomas Berry, *The Great Work: Our Way Into the Future* (New York: Random House, 2000).

13. Iain McGilchrist, *The Master and His Emissary: The Divided Brain and the Making of the Western World* (New Haven, CT: Yale University Press, 2009).

14. Anaïs Nin, *Seduction of the Minotaur* (Athens, OH: Swallow Press, 1961), 145.

15. Evelyn Fox Keller, *A Feeling for the Organism: The Life and Work of Barbara McClintock* (New York: Henry Holt, 1983), 198.

16. Fyodor Dostoevsky, *The Idiot*, trans. Richard Pevear and Larissa Volokhonsky (New York: Random House, 2001), 382.

17. Alfred North Whitehead, *Adventures of Ideas* (New York: Penguin, 1967), 324.

18. Henri Poincaré, *Science and Method* (Mineola, NY: Dover, 2003), 22; original work published 1914.

Chapter One

Contemplative Mind

Our thoughts first possess us. Later, if we have good heads, we come to possess them. [1]

—Ralph Waldo Emerson

At a conference not long ago, one of the speakers explained that he was involved with contemplative architecture. There was a silent pause in the large auditorium as his remark hung in the air. Most of us in the audience were groping around in our minds trying to imagine what he meant by this. Did it mean building meditation halls or religious buildings? Were the construction workers hammering nails in unison with eyes closed? He went on to explain that for him this meant designing a building with more space on the inside than there was on the outside. There was a long pause as we all took this in.

This image hints at a key direction for education in this extraordinary age. The greater the information, technology, and demands from the world around us, the more essential is our interiority, that is, the inner capacities for creativity, imagination, character, emotional balance, and more. To deal with the enormous complexity on the outside, we need a deep enough inner life.

We know the dominant Western approach to knowledge for the last several hundred years has been guided primarily by a quest for control, predictability, and comprehension of the external and material worlds, from the atom to the atmosphere. But throughout history, for some the quest for knowledge was also directed inward, exploring subjective experiences and how the mind works. These interior explorers have developed *inner technologies* to know and grow the mind directly. This direction of knowing we will call contemplative.

The contemplative has been used throughout the wisdom traditions as a key to developing the inner life and uncovering essential knowledge. It has found renewed value everywhere from religion to medicine and even in the military in the form of mindfulness practice, relaxation training for stress management, and more. Yet a contemplative way of knowing has been entirely absent from contemporary education, that is, until some recent initiatives have broken into schooling and are establishing a bona fide new field. [2] In the West the modernist episteme emphasizing attention to what is measurable, exterior, and material and a mind that is rational, categorical, and linear has elbowed the contemplative out of favor.

Historically, contemplative practices have included: meditation, which has endured for thousands of years in Buddhism; various forms of yoga from Hindu traditions; contemplative prayer in Christianity, such as that of St. Theresa of Avila; radical questioning through dialogue such as that expressed by Plato or the self-inquiry of Ramana Maharshi; metaphysical reflection of the Sufi tradition, which leads to the deeper intuitive insight of the heart (*qalb*); and the deep pondering suggested in the Jewish Kabbalah. Each of these approaches (alongside others) offers a means to interrupt habitual thought routines and deepen awareness. Even the roots of our own liberal arts include developing that interior life through contemplation. Ancient philosophy adopted breathing exercises, meditation on death, examination of conscience, and contemplation of nature in order to develop knowledge and knower. [3]

The contemplative complements rational and sensory knowing, providing an inner technology designed to expand awareness, shift states of consciousness, and watch the mind in action. Today, approaches, though often derived from spiritual traditions, need not impose any content or belief; they address *how* we know not *what* we should know and therefore pose little threat to secular classrooms.

While various practices may evoke different kinds of awareness, such as creative breakthrough or compassion, they share in common a typically nonlinear, nonrational way of knowing. Translated into classroom outcomes, opening the contemplative mind can engender concentration and awareness, critical reflection, emotional regulation, creative opening, and sensitivity.

A contemplative mind does not take away from literacy and numeracy, action or reasoning; it deepens our ability to engage and thus understand information and ourselves in context, in relationship, in our lives. What the contemplative mind offers education is not a different set of knowledge so much as an expanded approach to knowing, one that engenders:

- an *epistemology of presence* that moves past conditioned habits of mind to stay awake in the here and now.
- a more *intimate and integral empiricism* that includes in the consideration of the question a reflection on ourselves.

- a *pedagogy of resonance* that shapes our graciousness and spaciousness toward meeting and receiving the world nondefensively.
- a *deepened capacity for resilience*, calming and balancing body and emotions.
- an inner technology for *opening the aperture of consciousness.*

PRESENCE

Have you ever eaten a meal and realized that you really had not tasted any of it? Have you ever talked with someone, or maybe to a whole class, and realized that they were not really listening to you or you to them? If you have ever found yourself having just read several pages only to pause and realize that you had no idea what you just read, you know the importance of presence in learning and living. Through such experience we understand that in learning and in life, the *quantity* of time-on-task is subordinate to the *quality* of attention one brings to the task. If we are distracted, lost in thought, or shut off in some way it is very difficult to get the full measure and meaning of what is offered. But there is great pressure today that invites us not toward more depth, sensitivity, or presence but instead toward more distraction.

At a recent computer conference, Linda Stone, a former Apple and Microsoft executive, addressed her audience, a majority of whom, rather than looking at her, were looking down at their laps as she was speaking. They were working on their hand-held devices checking email and social media, texting, some were probably writing snarky notes about the speaker on a live blog, and who knows what else. She got their attention when she named a new "disorder"—continuous partial attention, or CPA.[4]

The demand quality of instant global communication and access to constant virtual stimulation can funnel life into rapidly changing sound bites, image bites, and data bytes. This steady pull on our attention prevents many of us from being able to give anything or anyone our full, undivided attention. It may also engender a sense of constant crisis. We are always on the lookout, always ready to respond with a swish or peck on something electronic. Our attention is here and there and everywhere, constantly interrupting itself and always on its way to somewhere else. No wonder the world of energy drinks, coffee franchises, and antianxiety medications has been doing so well. In this race without a finish line the goal is just to keep up, indefinitely.

Splintering our attention, multitasking and jumping to the next call, message, or sales pitch become increasingly the norm. To be sure, some situations really benefit from multitasking, and for some it provides welcome stimulation. And there are some advantages to functioning as live electronic nodes constantly plugged into the information superhighway; our ability to offload memory, access information, and be in communication is astounding. But there are downsides too. Like a dog whose attention is instantly captured by the squirrel trying to pass by, we can be taken for a fruitless run by anything and everything.

Stone suggested that talking to someone with CPA is like talking to someone at a cocktail party who is constantly on the lookout for the next, presumably better, conversation. The conversation does not get very far before their eye catches the next more interesting mark, and they are off. The result is that continuous availability actually inhibits our ability to really be available—that is, to meet another person or idea deeply and to give them or it our full, undivided attention. In this sense, constantly being accessible—a node on the information highway—ultimately makes us profoundly inaccessible.

It is hard to stay present when a constant stream of distractions vie for our attention—distractions not only from outside us—the message, the noisy neighbor—but especially from within. Thoughts and worries about the past or the future, about others or ourselves, seem to be desperately trying to get our attention—"Hey look at me!" Our nearly constant, restless, uncontrollable chatter has been referred to as *monkey mind*, as our minds jump from one thing to the next. We can also find ourselves stuck, looping around and around on the same thoughts.

However, we know at times our minds operate in other ways as well. The internal dialogue seems to ebb and flow; in some moments the chatter of the monkey mind recedes and another mode surfaces. Perhaps this occurs when we are entering or waking from a dream, during a good workout, when we experience an intuitive flash, during a moment of love or appreciation, when we are absorbed in an issue, or when nature, art, or beauty grabs our attention. Our capacity for presence can involve learning how to intentionally settle that internal chatter and in so doing invite a more spacious and gracious way of knowing.

From the voice of our primary grade teacher: "Okay class, pay attention" to our inner voice such as when we are trying to will ourselves to carry on with some work: "Concentrate!" perhaps the most fundamental injunction for learning is to pay attention. Yet we rarely help students to do this, we just insist that they do.

William James, the father of American psychology, thought this ability to shift awareness was extraordinarily important.

> The faculty of voluntarily bringing back a wandering attention, over and over again, is the very root of judgment, character, and will. An education which should improve this faculty would be *the* education *par excellence*. But it is easier to define this ideal than to give practical direction for bringing it about. [5]

At the beginning of the twentieth century, James was apparently not aware that so many wisdom traditions had already developed tried and true internal technologies specifically to develop the ability to focus, steady, sustain, and shift attention.

These technologies are readily available to us today. Most meditative or contemplative practice begins with intentionally shifting focus and concentrating on something—a word, an idea, the flow of thoughts and sensations, an image, or our breath.

> *We might, for example, simply try to bring our awareness to our breathing for several minutes, noticing its natural movement in and out. When we find our thoughts drifting, as they are so likely to do, bring our attention back to the breath. For some, counting 1-2-3-4 for the inhale and perhaps 1 to 8 for the exhale helps to maintain focus. But again we may find our attention wandering and again, without judgment, we bring our awareness back to the breath. If you find yourself thinking, distracted, working on a problem, don't fight it, don't get stuck in it, just note it and allow it and you to be for a moment and gently redirect your awareness back to your breath. Perhaps you can imagine those thoughts or concerns floating up like bubbles from under water. When they reach the surface they simply burst and disappear; and we return to the breath.*

In time such simple practice can develop the muscle of concentration and the sensitivity of awareness. The breath is used especially as a way of focusing attention, setting tempo, slowing down both body and mind to be more available to this moment. In various practices other focal points are offered, for example, concentrating on a word, phrase (e.g., "peace," "ocean," "let go"), or an image instead of breath. Further dimensions are sometimes added as we will see, such as an invitation to focus on compassion, but attention remains central.

This is pretty simple, in fact, so simple that it may be hard to see what all the fuss around contemplative practices is actually about. But developing the capacity for presence gives us power to direct, steady, and open our awareness intentionally, and this essentially helps us get out of our own way in order to tap both ourselves and the world at a greater depth.

Attention can become single-pointed in order to narrow in on a target such as concentrating on an activity, or it can be soft, open, and sensitive to the unexpected as when we see without any agenda taking in the whole scene. Here are two simple and easily modified exercises that invite deployment of attention and opening awareness or sensitivity.

> *Take a few deep breaths, bring yourself into a comfortable and relaxed position, closing your eyes completely or partially, whatever you feel comfortable doing. Take some time. What sounds, tastes, sensations, and so forth are available in the moment? Just notice and follow how you experience each. You*

might start with your attention outside you and then move inside to those
bodily sensations. Notice the subtleties of each.

Or this:

Making the intention and the effort to really look at, smell, taste, and feel our
food brings us into the present moment and opens the possibility for nourish-
ment beyond the vitamins and proteins. We might start with slowly eating a
single item, like a raisin, and give this our full attention as we soak in texture
and tastes, watching the sensations unfold.

Knowledge by Presence

Here is another way to speak of presence especially as it relates to learning:
presence opens knowing. Taking a page from the wisdom schools, the great
texts of the traditions are often described as *living words*: they are in some
mysterious way alive on the page. But the words, while right in front of us,
are not always so easy to comprehend. As living words, the implication is
that their meaning is somehow encrypted and compressed. This is why in all
of the traditions there is invitation to return to the words again and again in
order to see what light might be revealed this time around. To gain access to
the mysteries and reveal the meaning, we have to break the code.

The process of deep learning in a secular text or in knowing our neighbor
may actually not be so different. The biology text, the notes on the board, the
"text" that is the person or situation in front of us, and the world as a whole
are living words—awaiting expansion in order to be more fully understood,
more fully tasted, more nourishing. Their richness, beauty, and dimensional-
ity already exist here and now but must be decompressed to be realized. So
how do we break the code?

The secret lies in *knowledge by presence*, which involves looking not
only at the outer words or data but also opening into ourselves. The code is
broken, the words come alive, and the world is opened only through a corresponding opening of consciousness within us.

The instructions to return to the words again and again is an invitation to
enter into relationship with the symbols and signs and allow ourselves to
both open *to* them and be further opened *by* them. This is like a two-headed
key opening a series of locks that lead simultaneously into ourselves and into
the data. In this sense the symbol and the surface, whether a holy book or a
textbook, will disclose themselves only to the degree that we can open to
them. We might call this *reciprocal revelation*. This highlights that *what* we
know is bound to *how* we know.

RESILIENCE

In a class the other day I asked my students how many of them were feeling *frazzled;* they looked a bit harried. We did not discuss the meaning of the word but it seemed that everyone had some first-hand experience of what it meant. Nearly all said they felt this way today and regularly; it was the new normal for many. They described the typical sources of their frazzle as pressure to keep up with school, work outside of school both present and future, relationships with family and friends, as well as other particularities of their current life like a looming court date or family member's illness. For some it was as if they were trying to catch up to an accelerating train that was just out of reach and getting farther away with each passing second. Those bigger, longer-term concerns (e.g., "What will I do with my life?") also seemed to loom nearby, not like an exciting adventurous horizon but, for the vast majority, more like some high gravity force that was pressing down on their life. Feeling anxious, scattered, pressured, and easily distracted characterized this unsatisfying, off-kilter state. It is no news that this is common and maybe increasingly so among many.

As mentioned previously, young people are growing into a stressful world. In the United States, for example, the third leading cause of death for 10–14-year-olds is suicide; and the second and third leading causes of death for 15–24-year-olds are homicide and suicide, respectively.[6] Millions of children are on antidepressants, anti-anxiety medication, and more. An uncertain and rapidly changing job market, polarized political and social environments, and environmental catastrophe are all brought home through constant electronic stimulation that gives instant access not only to dizzying amounts of information but also to sex, violence, and sophisticated advertising.

During stress what has come to be referred to as the HPA axis (hypothalamus, pituitary, adrenal) coordinates autonomic nervous system response that gets us ready for fight or flight in part by increasing levels of the hormone cortisol, which is produced in the adrenal gland. But in an age of constant stimulation designed to grab our attention, shock us, or arouse us, not to mention the accelerated pace of the day, we may not return to an optimal baseline state, instead remaining in a constant state of frazzle. The hyperarousal of the HPA axis and elevated levels of cortisol have been related to obesity, memory deficit,[7] and even the neurobiology of suicide.[8] In general, we know that anxiety, depression, and significant levels of stress can impair mental processing and thus learning.

In and of itself the sheer volume and pace of information and the penchant for multitasking lead to a stress response. There is a limit to our working memory—the amount of information we can hold in our minds at any given time. When we approach that maximum—something that is not hard to do in multitasking—a response in the brain occurs that looks just like our response to other kinds of stress. We essentially lose some of our ability to think well.

In addition to the activity of the HPA axis, general brain activity shifts under stress. If we are agitated or frazzled in some way, the more primitive parts of the brain tend to dominate; essentially this means our emotional and instinctual survival responses are in high gear. When this happens, the cerebral cortex recedes in influence. The activity of the cortex helps coordinate sophisticated integration of thought, emotion, planning, meaning, empathy, compassion, executive function, and more. The basic idea is that when we are frazzled, the prefrontal cortex—the area most associated with higher-order processing, more creative and agile thinking, and executive control—basically goes offline. It also appears that sadness has a similar effect as frazzle.[9] Those higher brain centers are less involved in a state of sadness, and when this happens fresh possibility and flexibility contracts.

Attention, memory, learning, and performance are largely state dependent—that is, the states of body, mind, and emotions are central to learning. Reading comprehension, performance on the tennis court, or ability to play the flute depend not only on skill level but also on state of mind and body. The good news is that contemplative practice has been shown to reduce the level of cortisol during nonstressful events, increase response during stress, quicken the return to baseline levels,[10] and generally calm limbic (regions involved more with strong emotion) firing, thereby helping to bring the higher brain centers back on line.

One of the most well-established effects of contemplation is a change in physiological state, which in turn cascades into shifts in affect and cognition. For example, if we ring a bell, close eyes, and focus on our breath or a sense of love generally we send a signal throughout the body-brain system that decreases blood pressure, lowers heart rate, and reduces cortisol level. Such an immediate shift can have powerful influence on the ability to focus or be present in the classroom or on a task by reducing emotional frazzle and helping to quiet the habitual chatter of the mind. This shift in turn allows us to either lock on to material or consolidate freshly learned material, thereby avoiding retroactive interference (muddling up memory with the next material).

Stress response and the impact on learning can be quite general and can also be very particular. For a student who goes into vapor lock at the sight of a math problem (*"One train leaves Kansas City at 3:00pm traveling east-bound at 70 miles per hour, a second train leaves Omaha at 1:30 traveling west at 45 miles per hour . . ."*) shifts of state can dramatically change performance.

In a program many years ago I worked with students who had math anxiety. What we discovered was that their difficulty had little to do with deficit capacities toward math and nearly everything to do with the state of mind as they approached the problem. They had a very low frustration threshold toward math and would either leap into panic or drift into a kind of dissociative fog, "spacing out." What resolved their difficulty in a few class sessions was teaching some basic contemplative skills that helped them find the right state to avoid shutting down in an anxious reaction, and then providing some very basic one-on-one math coaching as needed. In this sense much of education may benefit from simultaneous training in both the right *skill* set and the right *mind-set*.

One of my daughters came home from elementary school one afternoon. As she was hoeing out her book bag I noticed a poor grade on a spelling test; she happened to be a very good speller and her grade was uncharacteristically low. "What happened on this one?" she was asked. She paused for just a second and recounted that her class had been working on math just before and that they had gone right into spelling; she said, "I still had my math head on." She recognized that there was no time for making the shift to a more useful mind-set.

Beverly, a second-grade teacher, regularly invited her students to take their shoes off and wiggle their toes in class in between various types of lessons like spelling and math to help shift their mind and body between activities. Of course the children loved doing this and Beverly could see that this simple ritual helped students to make the transition.

If our attention is scattered, racing, or on guard, we may have little capacity to be present. At the beginning or the end of a lesson or a study session, during a confusing or tense moment, at the start or end of the day, pausing in silence gives the mind a chance to prepare for or consolidate learning, transition between activities, and rebalance our minds.

Being able to shift out of being frazzled or recalibrate our current state— emotional regulation and focus—allows us to negotiate solutions and interactions more successfully. From a state of frazzle, sadness, anger, or anxiety it may be hard to see a clear way through problems. Basically, if we can find a way to avoid freaking out, overreacting, or being overwhelmed, we may avoid or overcome being frazzled. This allows more of us to be available, present and awake for what comes our way.

In addition to a shift in state, contemplative practice may also have an effect on long-term traits, such as emotional balance and resilience, allowing more stable access to our most important human capabilities.

For example, in one study of meditators whose practice involves "thoughtless awareness" or "mental silence" two groups were shown four brief video clips; three clips where "emotionally neutral" and one "emotionally negative" (an excerpt from Michael Haneke's film *Funny Games* in which two young people are abusing a family). The EEG data reflected in the meditators showed lower "arousal" and greater proneness to sustain "internal locus of attention."[11] Essentially the meditation group did not get carried away in a reactive state so easily, did not lose their "center," and were able to maintain a degree of openness and witnessing detachment. Impulse control problems, distractibility, road rage, violence on the playground, frustration, and tolerance are all affected by this capacity. In this sense such practice can provide, as T. S. Eliot said, a kind of "still point in a turning world."[12]

Intelligence of the Heart

With concerns of violence, bullying, anxiety, and more making the front pages, education's responsibility has included concerns of character and civility. If education is, in part, about growing our humanity, practices that are geared toward kindness or compassion may be worth exploring in the classroom. Of course this can be done in a way that crosses lines of church and state, for example, by imposing the image of particular religious figures, symbols, or concepts, but it can also be done in a way that is pretty universal. Here are two simple and inclusive practices that are safe and easy to employ.

> *Settle in quietly for a few moments. Invite your body to relax a bit, close your eyes if that is comfortable; let your chair and gravity do their jobs as you just notice your breath going gently in and out. As you relax bring your attention to the area of your chest, where you have experienced the feelings of love, care, or appreciation. Take a moment and bring to mind and heart someone or something that you genuinely feel appreciation for—something or someone you feel thankful for or that you love. Take a quiet moment to really bring it or them into view. Put yourself in the scene with them. What is the feeling? Do your best to really feel some of that right now for the next few moments. After a short while, now simply convey your appreciation, gratitude, or love toward them in some way. Feel appreciation and then find a way to send this along to them.*

Praying for the well-being of others is common across most wisdom traditions both East and West. Loving kindness, or *metta,* practice, from Buddhism, is a classic example of a very inclusive type of contemplation directing our intentions especially toward others. Basically, it begins with assuming a typically relaxed contemplative presence and repeating particular phrases inwardly. There are plenty of readily available examples out there of "loving kindness" meditation; here is the basic structure that moves from a request toward oneself, outward to loved ones, to others beyond one's circle, perhaps to those whom we have difficulty with, and eventually to all beings. You might vary the wording somewhat and the circles that you extend your intentions toward. For example, educators might include their students; others want to be certain to hold the earth itself in loving kindness. Holding an image or feeling of care toward others may help to embody this genuinely. Here are the phrases you repeat:

May I be safe and protected.
May I be peaceful and happy.
May I be healthy and strong.
May I find my way.

Continue repeating the phrases until you are comfortable, perhaps three times or many more. Next extend the circle outward toward a loved one, perhaps someone in your family, and again repeat three times (or perhaps more).

May he/she/they be safe and protected.
May he/she/they be peaceful and happy.
May he/she/they be healthy and strong.
May he/she/they find their way.

Next, extend the circle further, perhaps to a particular person or group (e.g., students, some refugees, a difficult person for you, humanity) or whom-ever. Bring that person or group to mind as best as possible with the help of images and feelings. The goal is not merely to say the words but instead to practice unconditional love toward ourselves and to all beings. We should not expect to be able to offer unconditional love to everyone initially, especially those with whom we have some lingering conflict or difficulty. To be aware or mindful of those feelings and honestly acknowledge those difficult spots is more fruitful that trying to force well wishes or do so disingenuously. Now choose a next group or person and continue the practice as above. In a limited time slot you might take three rounds, for example: self, loved ones, all of humanity, or vary as you think might be appropriate.

TRANSCENDENCE

Emerson's epigraph that begins this chapter ("Our thoughts first possess us. Later, if we have good heads, we come to possess them.")[13] acknowledges that there are times when our thoughts and feelings are in the driver's seat. Despite our best intentions, we end up down some path without having much say in the matter. We find ourselves caught in some mood or obsessing about something without realizing how we got there. Or despite our best efforts and intentions to study or finish some work, we find ourselves drifting far from that destination. Our hormones, blood sugar, last night's sleeplessness, our life circumstance, the adolescent brain, that phone call, and all manner of things push us in all sorts of directions. But Emerson hints that there is a way out of being taken for a ride, to transcend these limits of mind.

Transcendence is not a word that usually hangs around education, being more at home in religion. But understanding transcendence as a process or capacity of living systems to go beyond existing limitations makes this rele-vant for learning. Education can help us transcend our ignorance, our limita-tions, perhaps our primitive drives and strive for something greater as we seek what is good and true and beautiful. As humans we can transcend our circumstances, whether overcoming a disease like polio or a condition like poverty, through creativity, hard work, and a bit of grace perhaps. We may even help transcend things like oppression on a larger scale. Think: Gandhi or M. L. King Jr.

A rise in the belief in human transcendent agency took hold in the Renaissance. Following the rediscovery of ancient Greek texts and after the bubonic plague wiped out a quarter of the population of all of Europe, the value of human life became significantly reappraised. For example, Pico della Mirandola's *Oration on the Dignity of Man* celebrates the wonder of humanity, especially of human potential. The capacity that makes us most worthy of admiration, he contends, is precisely our ability to create what we are to be, to sow our own seeds from the gifts we have been given. Essentially, this shift gave new confidence in the human capability for agency and self-transcendence: internal and external, material and spiritual, geographic and economic. From Dante to da Vinci the Renaissance mind took flight.

By the way, this elevation of the person was not antispiritual but instead provided an expanded way of considering it; the "humanist" mind celebrated spirituality through much of the art, literature, and philosophy of the day. We might say that the spiritual could now come through us, not just exist beyond us.

In the West much of the attention on personal agency and transcendence has been about transcending external circumstances. We move westward, make our fortunes, secure our liberty, build our dreams, dam the river, smash the atom. However, the primary starting point for the contemplative mind is to pay attention not to the outside but instead to our interiority, noticing the quality and kind of our thoughts, feelings, and sensations. For the contemplative mind the capacity for transcendence can involve overcoming habitual patterns of mind and behavior in order to free us from a more limited view. We might say that the contemplative seeks to change nothing but the way we look at things.

The capacity for *witnessing* the contents of consciousness rather than merely reacting is a key. This permits us to inquire both into the question at hand and also toward the asker of the question. We can become both the object and the instrument of inquiry.

> *Where are you now? What are you aware of inside in this moment? Take a moment and notice what thoughts, feelings, sensations rise to the surface of awareness.*

If you are able to notice something then some part of you is doing the noticing and something was being noticed. We can make a distinction between the "me"—the thoughts, feelings, sensations, and images that are the content of consciousness—and the "I"—that part of us that is able to notice. This witnessing or watching is a key to Emerson's promise.

When we are caught in any strong emotion or constricting thought it can feel all-consuming. Witnessing what is going on helps us rise just above the turbulent waves of mind, giving us a little distance between us and the sensation, thought, or feeling so that we have a chance to play and work with it without being instantly overwhelmed.

The practice usually involves just noticing without judgment whatever emerges in the mind. At the start of a lesson or at any point in the day, we might invite students (and ourselves) to:

> *Take a few deep breaths and then just notice your breath for a few moments. Close your eyes if you are comfortable doing so, and tune in to where you are right in this moment. Once you are settled in, ask yourself the following question: "Where am I now?" Allow whatever impressions to arise as you hold the question "Where am I now?" Are you thinking about the day ahead? Rehashing some past experience? How much of you is: in your body? in your head? outside you? stuck in a painful nook? Does an answer emerge about where you are on the path of your life? Just be aware for a few moments, noticing where you are and how that feels.*
>
> *Don't get attached to the content, don't push it away, just watch it arise, acknowledge it, and return to your watching. After a few moments in a classroom we might ask students to take two minutes and share their experience with the person next to them (or in their notebook) or with the class as a whole.*

This allows us to observe the activity of our minds rather than simply being captured by its content. Such awareness allows us to recognize, inquire into, and also potentially interrupt usual patterns of thinking and impulsivity, freeing the mind for insights. For example, instead of just seething with anger, the contemplative mind may allow a little more space between the anger and us. We might both have our anger and also notice it: "I'm really angry; what's that about?" rather than simply being lost to the anger. This does not mean that we feel less, but instead there is more interior spaciousness, more room to both have the sensation and to notice it. In so doing we are more able to dis-identify with the contents that so often seem to define us.

We can also change that focal length like adjusting the lens on a camera. At times there may be value in coming in close to really experience whatever is happening (e.g., "What exactly is that feeling and where is it in my body?" "What is the thought behind this?"). Other times we benefit from stepping back (e.g., "What is the big picture here?").

This simple practice could be extended into a daily activity in or outside of class. Instead of checking our electronics at any free opportunity, thinking "Where am I now?" might become a habit of checking in with ourselves. After having been introduced to this simple practice, some students report that they find themselves doing this regularly. The greater the demands from outer technology, the greater the need there is for this kind of inner technology to help us notice and balance our minds.

When applied repeatedly such witnessing allows us to notice habitual patterns of how our mind operates. For example, are we often thinking about the next thing we have to do or regularly feel like we are racing ahead rather than attending to the moment at hand? Are we quick to reject certain ideas or people, or always driven by certain presuppositions or unchecked assumptions—for example, "Math is too hard for me" or "I don't like people like that"—that we have mistakenly taken as fact?

In learning, this process of self-inquiry includes monitoring our own understanding. For example, if a student is trying to decide whether she understands the text she has just read or whether she has learned material sufficient for an upcoming exam, she can step back and use one part of her awareness to inquire into another part. She might ask: "Do I understand this?" "How would I answer a particular question?" "How might I explain this to someone else?" "Does my paper say what I want it to?" and so forth as a kind of internal dialogue or self-inquiry. This simple procedure enabled by the mind witnessing itself is hugely helpful for comprehension of material.

In addition, this metacognizing—noticing the content and the patterns of our thought process—can take us even further. It gives us the ability to step back and inquire more fundamentally into our preexisting knowledge, the lens through which we see the world. For example, a doctoral student writes out her conceptual baggage—what she assumes and knows, her motivation and hopes—about her topic. Younger students describe what they already know and believe about a subject that is in the queue for study. In both of these simple examples, this helps us step outside and reflect on the lens through which we are looking. In so doing we have a chance to expose presuppositions and prejudice and to deconstruct positions of role, belief, culture, and so forth in order to see more deeply or from multiple perspectives. This allows students the conceptual flexibility to transcend their own limits of knowledge by which they come to see the world.

Witnessing the content of our consciousness, whether our emotional state or our understanding of the lesson at hand, is a fundamental capacity underlying both emotional maturity and deepened cognition. It allows us to use the mind rather than being used by it.

A NEW VIEW

Our mind and body serve as portals through which the world enters. One of the functions of the mind is actually to serve as a reducing valve. To some extent we are prewired to hear a certain range of noise, and this is different from the range that our dog hears. Our socialization constructs further filters that help us distinguish, label, and categorize our experiences: "This is an oak tree; that's a holly bush." In this sense our mind arranges (or assimilates, as Piaget said) our experience through previous associations and interpretations. This categorical understanding provides a kind of shorthand—"That is dangerous," "This is a friend," and so forth—that is valuable for sorting information, a capacity essential for survival and for managing the volume of input available to us. But with this categorical way of knowing we have difficulty seeing things freshly and flexibly, qualities of knowing that are essential for adaptation, innovation, creativity, and solving novel problems.

Neuroscientist Walter J. Freeman's study of the brain uncovered that often something entirely unexpected occurs when we are confronted with new information or stimulation. What happens is that the neural activity due to sensory stimuli essentially disappears in the cortex.[14] That means we are not really taking in what we sense. Some stimulation, like the sight of a car heading our way or the sound of our partner's complaint once again, flows into the brain, and it appears to evoke in its place an internal pattern, which the mind uses to represent the external situation. We think we see the real world, but we actually see what is already in our minds, based on memory and expectations. If we are not aware of the power of these internal models, we may just accept what we think we see as reality and become dependent upon them rather than open to new input. (Freeman may be describing a characteristic response of the brain's left hemisphere, whereas the right is more available for fresh encounter; but whatever the physical substrate, the function is the key.)[15] In the face of a new situation the categorical mind tends to replay the maps in our head rather than seeing the landscape in front of us.

But we have the capacity to modify this habitual categorical process and in so doing open the mind. The possibility of schooling is not just to load us up but also especially to open us up. In addition to developing the ability to hold and deploy attention and to witness the flow of our consciousness, contemplative practices invite a kind of opening and receptivity. This state of mind may result in a flow of ideas, breakthrough insight, or a larger perspective. Optimally, the categorical and the contemplative work together, our awareness oscillating back and forth between our category and a more direct or fresh encounter, which in turn may reshape our categories, and on and on. However, without this opening for encounter we become dependent on predetermined categories and miss the opportunity for contact with the world.

The most daunting philosophic and scientific problem today is arguably that of explaining consciousness: What is consciousness? Where does it come from? How does it operate?

The prevailing assumption has been that our individual brain *generates* consciousness. Some neurotransmitters activate and we have a thought. But this does not explain our experience, intention, or much else, however well it maps some of the mechanisms of the brain. It certainly does not account adequately for subjectivity, creativity, breakthrough, genius, or intention, and it does not reasonably explain those difficult problems of well-documented cases of near-death states where perception or other experience is recorded without brain activity, alleged past-life recollections where factually verifiable information has no reasonable conventional source, or legitimate psi and related phenomena, experiences where individuals seem to have connected with or received information that in some way defies neurobiochemical generation.

Another theory of consciousness was initially described more than one hundred years ago as a "transmission" model by William James and "filter" model by F. W. H. Myers and is receiving renewed interest today. [16] Basically the idea is that consciousness is not merely a by-product of individual brain activity but may exist as some field outside the body itself. In this sense we tap or receive it in some way. This does not discount the role of the brain, but it does not reduce consciousness to it. Among their many tasks, the mechanisms of the brain filter and receive consciousness.

There is not space here to elaborate this in any detail. And since consciousness does remain a profound mystery, we need not make any final commitments to a model of mind. At this point it may be most reasonable to understand the mind as both generating consciousness and receiving it. At least this seems consistent with our lived experience.

Artists and authors, scientists and inventors so often describe their process of insight and breakthrough as getting out of their own way, allowing something to flow through or to them, seemingly arising beyond direct control. We may recognize those moments when some fresh awareness breaks through in the shower or on a walk or other times when we are relaxed from our normal chain of thinking. Ancient Athenian philosopher Philo described his own inspirational breakthroughs in this way: "I have approached my work empty and suddenly become full, the ideas falling from a shower from above and being sown invisibly." [17] Accounts such as this are quite common in the experience of creativity and inspiration. [18] And while we do not need to make any ontological claims about the source (the brain, our muse, or whatever) we can keep our eyes on the process.

These moments do occur spontaneously, but certain ways of mind can be useful in wooing and welcoming consciousness in this direction regardless of whether we assume it is generated or received. In addition to focusing in on a question or problem, it is the mind's ability to stay open that is key.

While the practice of mindfulness can be powerfully useful in watching and witnessing our own mind in action, letting the mind just stay wide open helps us to be available to its own undirected flow of consciousness, which has been related to improved creativity [19] and improved implicit memory (the kind of memory that happens beneath our conscious awareness, such as when we learn to ride a bicycle, read facial expressions, or speak grammatically). [20]

What is central here is that minds are optimized for creativity and insight by balancing intention and surrender, holding steady and letting go, focusing and allowing.

The principle of openness and receptivity is a familiar way of knowing across the wisdom traditions. For example, in Zen Buddhism, this attitude or way of seeing is called "beginner's mind." It means being open to the world, appreciating and meeting it with fresh eyes—just watching it (and ourselves) without preset expectations or categories.

Rather than willing or forcing something to occur, this aspect of the contemplative opens willingness or receptivity; in a sense we are creating "soft mind"[21] or "a soft spot to sprout it."[22] Going to the university curriculum committee or to the school board and advocating for "soft mind" might be met with a little skepticism, but this open, flexible, receptive, "soft" consciousness that is so essential for discovery and creativity balances the "hard" critical intellect important for framing the question and analyzing and translating outcomes.

While the world is abuzz with noise, from the whir of our surroundings to our portable and private playlists to the internal chatter of our thoughts, silence and stillness are allies of the contemplative mind, opening awareness to more subtle currents of consciousness. Rumi said it this way:

> There is a way between voice and
> presence where information flows.
> In disciplined silence it opens.
> With wandering talk it closes. [23]

Notice the phase "disciplined silence." This is not merely passivity or relaxation; it requires a certain relaxed wakefulness. Gowan makes the point this way: "When Michelangelo did the Sistine Chapel he painted both the major and the minor prophets. They can be told apart because, though there are cherubim at the ears of all, only the major prophets are *listening.*"[24] This presence opens us to the world and the world to us.

Although it can sound pretty simple, staying awake in this way is not necessarily automatic. As psychologist Rollo May suggested, "The deeper aspects of awareness are activated to the extent that the person is committed to the encounter."[25] Rollo May goes on to say that this engagement must be followed, not simply with a caffeinated buzz—a particular kind of wakefulness—but instead a receptivity, "hold[ing] . . . [oneself] alive to hear what being may speak. . . . [This] requires a nimbleness, a fine-honed sensitivity in order to let one's self be the vehicle of whatever vision may emerge."[26] Awareness is a natural gift that can be refined and expanded or numbed and shut down. Developing contemplative ways of knowing involves both this

concentration (intention, focus) on the one hand, and the receptivity (empty-
ing, allowing, letting go) on the other.

Simply making space for unfocused silence, whether through a little nap-
time, daydream, inviting the mind to wander, spontaneous doodling, or other
"mindless" activity can provide a healthy complement to our earnest focused
attention.

> *Sit or lie down, be silent and just "not do." You are welcome and safe here.*
> *Nothing to do, nothing to get right, feel free to let your body unwind and your*
> *mind wander. Take your time. Allow gravity to do its job and the chair or*
> *ground beneath you to support you without any effort on your part. Just let go*
> *and allow yourself to be silent and not do for a few minutes.*

The contemplative mind is brought forward not only through silence and
stillness but can find its way through our language that is at the center of
schooling.

Writing involves vision and revision: generation of ideas and then editing
or crafting. These require two different and complementary cognitive opera-
tions, but sometimes they get muddled together in practice in a way that
inhibits the generation of ideas; like driving a car with one foot pressing on
the gas pedal and one on the brake, it may be hard to get rolling. A process
approach to writing[27] may serve as a contemplative act as we bring both the
focus of our intention and the freedom of our spontaneous flow of ideas to
the task. For example, we might invite students to

> *take a few deep breaths, relax, and go inside for a few moments. When you are*
> *ready and with eyes opened, write everything you possibly can about a partic-*
> *ular topic (perhaps a class assignment, a reaction to the day's reading assign-*
> *ment, a current event, an upcoming paper, a personal situation, or whatever*
> *comes to mind). Let the feelings, the insight, the struggle, ideas, or whatever*
> *emerge and flow onto the paper. Write the heart of what you want to say. Free*
> *write it, with no concern for spelling, grammar, judgment, or logical coher-*
> *ence. Just go with the flow. What wants to come through? If you are not sure*
> *where to start, write, "I'm not sure where to start," and keep writing. You*
> *have ten minutes (or whatever limited time frame you have available).*
>
> *Afterward, read your work silently, suspend your critic, and just be curi-*
> *ous about what has been written. Then find one sentence, idea, feeling, or even*
> *a single word that stands out and serves as a trailhead for more. Take that*
> *sentence or idea or feeling as a new start and write freely for another five*
> *minutes, seeing where the trail leads next. You might try one more round,*
> *reading and then writing. Then, perhaps, you can: a) reflect on your process*
> *with a partner and/or b) read a sentence or a few sentences to your partner.*
> *Partners could practice just listening with curiosity and noting what stood out*
> *to them.*

There are a wide range of other practices—from creative visualization to walking in nature, from metaphysical pondering to poetry—that help bring the contemplative mind to life in schooling, whether with our youngest charges or in higher education. [28] A helpful "tree" (along with other information) listing a very wide range of contemplative possibilities is available at the Center for Contemplative Mind in Society, [29] and a wide array of various resources and programs in contemplative teaching and learning can be found at The Garrison Institute. [30]

Ultimately though, it is not exactly the methods themselves that are key, however helpful and even catalyzing they may be at times. Their job is to help us shift, witness, open, and maybe welcome something to us. Michel de Salzmann makes the point this way:

> For many years we try methods, but then at moments, there is enough energy for a sensitivity to appear and then for this Intelligence to appear. It is not methods that produce it. It's letting everything be, inside, just as it is, and opening to the attention. [31]

A turn toward a more integrative and contemplative mind begins with a teacher taking notice of his or her own inner life and then finding ways to invite students to do the same. While the change pivots on an instant, for it to be sustained and supported in schooling we will need to regain a vision of education large enough to attend to more than test scores, and use pedagogy that understands that the way we know affects what we know.

The contemplative mind develops our capacity for presence and openness, provides inner balance and resilience, grows the ability for witnessing and metacognition, and opens the mind for creativity and to transcend current limits of consciousness.

Its potential for growing the mind is both very practical (especially when we think of basics like concentration and the effects of stress on learning) and profound when we develop the ability to transcend our habits of mind and heart. At the most basic level, skill set or knowledge set—the predominant emphasis in schooling—is dependent largely on the *mind-set* that one brings to the task. The simple but subtle ability to intentionally witness, deploy, open, and shift attention is both an outcome of contemplative inquiry and the most fundamental mind skill needed for learning.

NOTES

1. Quoted in Merton M. Sealts, *Emerson on the Scholar* (Columbia, MO: University of Missouri Press, 1992), 257.

2. For a searchable database especially for K–12 education programs, see The Garrison Institute, www.garrisoninstitute.org/contemplative-education-program-database. For further re-

sources especially for higher education see: The Center for Contemplative Mind in Society, www.contemplativemind.org.

3. Pierre Hadot, *Philosophy as a Way of Life: Spiritual Exercises from Socrates to Foucault,* ed. Arnold I. Davidson, trans. Michael Chase (Malden, MA: Blackwell, 1995), 107.

4. Steven Levy, "(Some) attention must be paid!," *Newsweek* 148, no. 16 (March 2006).

5. William James, *The Principles of Psychology,* vol. 1 (New York: Henry Holt and Company, 1890), 424.

6. National Center for Injury Prevention and Control, "10 Leading Causes of Death, United States—2010," *Centers for Disease Control and Prevention,* accessed January 29, 2014, http://www.cdc.gov/injury/wisqars/pdf/10LCID_All_Deaths_By_Age_Group_2010-a.pdf.

7. Jacob Raber, "Detrimental Effects of Chronic Hypothalamic-Pituitary-Adrenal Axis Activation: From Obesity to Memory Deficits," *Molecular Neurobiology* 18, no. 1 (1998): 1–22.

8. J. F. López, D. M. Vázquez, D. T. Chalmers, and S. J. Watson, "Regulation of 5-HT Receptors and the Hypothalamic-Pituitary-Adrenal Axis: Implications for the Neurobiology of Suicide," *Academy of Science* 29, no. 836 (1997): 106–134.

9. Amy Arnsten, "The Biology of Being Frazzled," *Science* 280 (1998): 1711–1713.

10. C. R. MacLean, K. G. Walton, S. R. Wenneberg, D. K. Levitsky, J. P Mandarino, R. Waziri, S. L. Hillis, and R. H. Schneider, "Effects of the Transcendental Meditation Program on Adaptive Mechanisms: Changes in Hormone Levels and Responses to Stress After 4 Months of Practice," *Psychoneuroendocrinology* 22, no. 4 (1997): 277–295.

11. L. Aftanas and S. Golosheykin, "Impact of Regular Meditation Practice on EEG Activity at Rest and During Evoked Negative Emotions," *International Journal of Neuroscience* 115 (2005): 893–909.

12. Thomas S. Eliot, *Four Quartets* (New York: Harcourt, Brace, and World, 1971), 16.

13. Quoted in Sealts, *Emerson*, 257.

14. Walter J. Freeman, "The Physiology of Perception," *Scientific American* 264, no. 2 (1991): 78–85.

15. Iain McGilchrist, *The Master and His Emissary: The Divided Brain and the Making of the Western World* (New Haven, CT: Yale University Press, 2010).

16. Edward F. Kelly, Emily Williams Kelly, Adam Crabtree, Alan Gauld, Bruce Greyson, and Michael Grosso, *The Irreducible Mind: Toward a Psychology for the 21st Century* (Lanham, MD: Rowman & Littlefield, 2007).

17. Abraham J. Heschel, *The Prophets* (New York: Harper and Row, 1962), 333.

18. Tobin Hart, "Inspiration: An Exploration of the Experience and Its Meaning," *Journal of Humanistic Psychology* 38, no. 1 (1998): 7–35.

19. Benjamin Baird et al., "Inspired by Distraction: Mind Wandering Facilitates Creative Incubation," *Psychological Science* 23, no. 10 (2012): 1117–1122.

20. As reported in Dan Hurley, "Breathing In vs. Spacing Out," *The New York Times,* last modified January 23, 2014, http://www.nytimes.com/2014/01/19/magazine/breathing-in-vs-spacing-out.html?_r=0; Georgetown University Medical Center, "Mindfulness Inhibits Implicit Learning—The Wellspring of Bad Habits," *Georgetown University,* November 12, 2013, http://explore.georgetown.edu/news/?ID=73187&PageTemplateID=295.

21. Shunryu Suzuki, *Zen Mind, Beginner's Mind: Informal Talks on Zen Meditation and Practice* (New York: Weatherhill, 1970).

22. Mary Caroline Richards, *Centering in Pottery, Poetry, and the Person* (1962; repr., Hanover, NH: Wesleyan University Press, 1989), 63.

23. Jalāl ad-Dīn Muhammad Rūmī, *The Essential Rumi,* trans. C. Barks with J. Moyne, A. J. Arberry, and R. Nicholson (San Francisco: Harper San Francisco, 1995), 109.

24. John C. Gowan, "Creative Inspiration in Composers," *The Journal of Creative Behavior* 11, no. 4 (1977): 249–255.

25. Rollo May, *The Courage to Create* (New York: Bantam Books, 1975), 46.

26. Ibid., 91.

27. Peter Elbow, *Writing With Power: Techniques for Mastering the Writing Process* (New York: Oxford University Press, 1998).

28. Tobin Hart, "Opening the Contemplative Mind In Education," *Journal of Transformative Education* 2, no. 1 (2004).

29. You can find it at: www.contemplativemind.org/practices/tree.

30. You can find it at: www.garrisoninstitute.org.

31. Michel de Salzmann as cited in Fran Shaw, "Notes on the Next Attention," *Parabola* 36, no. 1 (2011): 92.

Chapter Two

Empathic Mind

The greatest of human discoveries in the future will be the discovery of human intimacy with all those other modes of being that live with us on this planet, inspire our art and literature, reveal that numinous world whence all things come into being, and with which we exchange the very substance of life.

—Thomas Berry [1]

How do we know a thing? Throughout time and culture the most essential knowing in many traditions has been described as coming through the heart and not the head: this was the eye of the soul for Plato, the eye of the Tao, the Chinese *hsin,* which is often translated as "mind" but includes both mind and heart. Author Antoine de Saint-Exupéry's Little Prince says it this way: "Here is my secret. It's quite simple: One sees clearly only with the heart. Anything essential is invisible to the eyes." [2] Somehow the heart is supposed to take us past self-interest and self-separateness to a deeper knowing. But beyond remembering to share and learning to play well with others, important to be sure, does the heart really have anything to offer education in a high-tech, high-test, information-laden world?

As we have named already, the common way we are trained to know through contemporary education tends to invite categorical identification rather than intimate meeting of the subject. This is largely because of a materialist worldview and along with it the domination of the assumptions of contemporary science, which are based largely on objectification. [3] The notion of objective knowing has led to a new level of control over the natural world, and its presuppositions have deluged educational practice. Cartesian subject-object division provides the cornerstone. This objectivist, reductionist, materialist knowing is wholly legitimate and valuable, but also wholly incomplete. Knowing in this way has consequences; it is an abbreviator's approach, in da Vinci's words, and abbreviation by its very definition misses some things.

The root meaning of the term *objective* is "standing against" or apart from. Educational leader Parker Palmer describes the consequence of this way of knowing:

> This image uncovers another quality of modern knowledge: it puts us in an adversary relationship with each other and our world. We seek knowledge in order to resist chaos, to rearrange reality, or to alter the constructions others have made. We value knowledge that enables us to coerce the world into meeting our needs—no matter how much violence we must do. Thus our knowledge of the atom has brought us into opposition to the ecology of earth, to the welfare of society, to the survival of the human species itself. Objective knowledge has unwittingly fulfilled its root meaning: it has made us adversaries of ourselves. [4]

With the distance between knower and known maintained and without recognition of their interplay, we remain separate from the world we perceive. The modernist objectification of the other, including the natural world (environment and body), contributes to difficulties in relationships and limits the experience from which to make ethical choices. At the beginning of the twentieth century, William James recognized that "materialism and objectivism" tend to lead human beings to see their world as alien. And "the difference between living against a background of foreignness [i.e., treating the world as alien] and one of intimacy means the difference between a general habit of wariness and one of trust."[5] Habitual wariness and distance engenders anxiety, depersonalization, alienation, and narcissism—those very personal problems of consciousness we find so prevalent today.

The maintenance of this separation between observer and observed is artificial, justified in the name of objectivity and reinforced by a cognitive repression of the awareness of interconnection. The problem is not the valuable arm's-length perspective that the intellect can provide; instead, the difficulty is the inflation and institutionalization of this approach that ends up reducing the world to a collection of objects. Today, as we shall see, these presuppositions are not only limiting; they are simply inconsistent with the most updated understanding of how the world, including our consciousness, operates.

INTIMATE EMPIRICISM

There are ways of knowing that involve a more intimate empiricism, one in which we lean into the object of inquiry, whether we are looking at a proton, a plant, or a person. This way of knowing seeks to make contact rather than simply categorize.

As a young woman Jane Goodall was asked by paleoanthropologist Richard Leakey to discover what she could learn about chimpanzees, human's nearest relatives. Leakey believed that such study could yield valuable information about human evolution. Goodall was game and entered the African forest with a long-standing passion toward animals, a conviction that they were interesting as individuals, and, significantly, without any formal training. Her field method was simply to get as close as she could and observe, giving the animals her full attention.

In time she did indeed come in close, sitting among them day after day as the chimpanzees gradually came to trust her presence. She began to see skills, social patterns, and more that up to that time no one had noticed or been able to witness. She discovered that chimpanzees used and modified tools, ate meat, demonstrated acts of compassion, and had language and complex social patterns. Her observations changed the way we see chimpanzees and the animal kingdom at large. It also has helped change the way we see ourselves.

Goodall balanced careful objective observation with connection, even love, as she describes. Naturalist Sy Montgomery explains Goodall's approach in this way. "Jane's strength is that she relinquished control . . . [this] allowed her to see and inspired her to stay."[6] Control is, of course, both the means and the goal of the scientific method: control of variables in experiments, control and predictability of natural forces. Yet Goodall's method was to come into relationship instead of control, to participate instead of manipulate. Montgomery suggested that Leakey himself described their task as both a scientific one and a spiritual one: "Theirs was a profoundly sacred journey to the brink of the chasm that modern man has carved between himself and the animals and, once there, to peer over its edge and perhaps, if they dared, to cross."[7]

The result of this empathic connection was profound insight, and something more. Goodall says that her method—the watching, the silence, the companionship—gave a "peace that reached into the inner core of my being."[8] This way of knowing has led her from primatology to humanitarianism, advocating for conservation and organizing to help ease poverty in Africa. She won the prestigious Kyoto Prize in basic science, and in 2002 the United Nations named her a Messenger for Peace. The way we know affects knowledge and love.

The move of the empathic mind is very simple and subtle; it takes place when we lead with curiosity instead of judgment, when we make contact instead of categories, when we appreciate and feel into, when we open to the encounter rather than defend against it, when we do not try to get anything but simply meet what is before us. It occurs from listening deeply, from communion rather than calculation, from genuinely meeting.

Philosopher Martin Buber described this shift as a movement from an "I-It" relationship toward one of "I and Thou."[9] Understanding comes when we empathize with the other and suspend our distant self-separateness for a moment. As we do so, recognition of interconnection may emerge. Vietnamese Buddhist monk Thich Nhat Hanh calls the activity "pure recognition," by which he means seeing without judgment, being aware with a kind of radical, nonjudgmental, childlike openness.[10]

Empathic knowing does not involve doing something to another person, animal, or object directly; instead a space is created in which we may participate with and open to one another. Meeting takes place in a kind of "clearing," as Heidegger named it,[11] or in "the between,"[12] in Buber's words, a space created by the kind of openness, sensitivity, and willingness that Goodall demonstrates.

Nobel laureate Barbara McClintock made remarkable discoveries in genetics that took years to unravel. When asked about her scientific process, she said, "You have to have a feeling for the organism. . . . You have to have an openness to let it come to you."[13] The organisms with which she worked were not chimpanzees or mice that you could imagine some kind of responsive relationship with; instead, she worked with corn, which was hard to get a smile or a squeak out of. The key to her astounding and extremely advanced understanding of genetics was, as she described, "the openness to let it come to you." She claimed that this attitude of openness and sensitivity, or "feeling for the organism," was the primary instrument of discovery.

While the analytic mind tends to *hold*, categorize, cut, and reform the world, the empathic mind and heart tend to *behold* it. When we see a piece of art or an incredible blue sky we may be captured by it for a moment; we just seem to be in a kind of frequency lock. We get in sync, in tune, and arrive at some understanding. The word *understanding* means literally "to stand under or among." This is participative knowing, quite a different and complementary way of knowing than the objectivity and critical reason that we have come to associate with science.

When we assimilate a tree or a flower (or person or idea), we anchor our attention first in our concept of the tree as we categorize and calculate: "What kind of tree is it?" "How old?" "What is its utility (shade, hardwood)?" "How big a chain saw would I need to cut it down; will it fall on the house if I do?" "Is it healthy?" "Who planted it?" This can be valuable information, but it is only part of the story. Instead of anchoring in the concept of the tree, we attempt to meet the tree itself. This may begin with an attitude of curiosity that leads into appreciation and develops into a feeling of affection, understanding, care, and even awe. As religionist Abraham Heschel wrote:

The loss of awe is the great block to insight. A return to reverence is the first prerequisite for a revival of wisdom. . . . Wisdom comes from awe rather than from shrewdness. It is evoked not in moments of calculation but in moments of being in rapport with the mystery of reality. The greatest insights happen to us in moments of awe. [14]

The empathic mind allows us to begin to see from multiple points of view, to share and learn from one another's tribe rather than just defend our own. This is the complement to critical reasoning or examination. To get to know the other, take up their position, see through their eyes—whether a person or a plant—engages the empathic heart as a legitimate and complementary source of knowledge. Heschel underscores just how important this is: "Mankind will not perish from want of information; but only want of appreciation."[15]

We open toward the other when we try to take the other's perspective. Simply trying to imagine what another being is experiencing can open the door. Ruth Shlossman, the principal at a private elementary school, describes a moment at her school:

When we had a new student who barely spoke English enter our school, I asked the students to imagine what it might be like for them if they suddenly had been placed in a school in Thailand or Nigeria or Italy, and what they might have hoped for in the way of kindness and support from fellow students and teachers in that situation. After a lively discussion of their fantasies and fears, I asked them to apply that to the new student attending our school. They got it.[16]

Even the most basic requirement of learning at every level, remembering, is enhanced by the empathic mind. A series of studies have demonstrated that we may remember best when we encode memory socially. In one of several similar studies, participants were asked to read statements describing everyday kinds of experiences. They were told that there would be a memory test on what they read. The second group of participants also read the same passages. However, they were told not to try to memorize the material but instead "form an overall impression of what the person who performed these various actions is like." Both groups were then tested to see what they could remember about what they had read. Though the second group was neither told that they would have a memory test nor to try to remember what they had read, those participants, those individuals who were asked to think empathically (i.e., "What is this person like?") did better on the memory test in study after study.[17] Social encoding led to better memory.

Because we are so strongly evolved for social connection, the empathic brain and mind are a natural aid to learning. When we hear the story of a subject rather than its bits and bytes we more naturally learn it. While a history class, for example, is often presented as the *what* and the *how*, it is the *why*—the human drama—that helps us engage it and give a more dynamic, realistic, human context.[18] In any subject the living story brings material to life in a way our mind can absorb naturally.

When we stretch past our self-separateness and self-interest to meet the other, communication can deepen to a genuine sense of community and communion. From the global economy to global warming we come to understand and experience the world as interdependent, and therefore our satisfaction and very survival depends on the quality of our relations. At no time in history has this been so apparent and so urgent.

FROM CATEGORY TO CONNECTION [19]

Our approach to learning and knowing, naturally, should be consistent with our best understanding of how our world and our minds work.

In its barest form, the modernist worldview is that the universe consists largely of individual units of inert matter and living individual agents acting from self-interest. From this point of view an objectivist, reductionist, materialist way of knowing seems reasonable. But our understanding of our world is radically and profoundly changing. We are increasingly recognizing our world as a living universe and persons as existing in and as a complex web of relations and influence.

In everything from physics to business, there is a fundamental change in worldview afoot. From melting ice caps to economic meltdowns we are beginning to understand the degree to which we are interconnected. We are coming to take for granted the realities of environmental systems and global economies, and these systems operate at even more fundamental levels helping us see just how interconnected we are. The world of quantum physics, where many of our conventional assumptions about how the world operates get turned on their heads, provides support and, as the physics-of-the-day often does, metaphor for a radically interconnected universe.

For example, nonlocality, the phenomenon that objects across the globe and the universe are somehow connected, provides a clear demonstration. The quantum world apparently does not operate on the kind of mechanical cause-and-effect principle that Sir Isaac Newton elaborated but instead demonstrates immediate and simultaneous change across time and space. What this implies is that the entire universe is interconnected at the most fundamental level that we can observe. This challenges the "local realistic" view of the universe that dominates conventional understanding. This "locality" assumption says that physical effects—for example, your voice—propagate over distance at a certain finite speed and diminish with distance. The high limit of this local phenomenon, according to Einstein's principles, is that nothing can travel faster than the speed of light. But quantum nonlocality demonstrates something quite different. At the quantum level, phenomena occur virtually simultaneously across great distance. Repeated laboratory experiments demonstrate that particles that at some point occupied the same state remain connected or correlated with each other over time and space. That is, when the state of one particle is changed, say electron spin, the other particle instantly changes in the same way even if they are on opposites sides of the globe. The bottom line: connection even at a distance.

The "reality" aspect of the "local realistic" view assumes that objects have characteristics intrinsic to them. However, quantum reality demonstrates that the characteristics of things, like the state of particles, are linked to and even created by the state of other things. These states are even influenced by our looking at them, as Heisenberg's uncertainty principle demonstrates.

Quantum physicist David Bohm, who by the way was a great integrator of science and spirituality, spoke about the *implicate order* and the *explicate order* as a way of making sense of the quantum world.[20] Essentially, the explicate is the material form governed generally by rules of space and time. The implicate implies a "hidden" or deeper level or system of reality, a force that connects all things. For Bohm, within the implicate order everything is interconnected; and, in principle, any individual element could reveal information about every other element in the universe. Bohm saw an "unbroken wholeness of the totality of existence as an undivided flowing movement without borders."[21] He believed that this not only applied to quantum physics but also was an appropriate way to see human consciousness.

From another realm of study anthropologist Gregory Bateson described the "pattern that connects."[22] Bateson fought against the reductionism of everything to matter and sought to reintroduce mind back into science and understanding of the world. In Bateson's view we could say that relation always codefines an object. Nothing exists on its own; in a psychological sense, we are always a self-in-relation. Bohm and Bateson imply that there are deep structures and patterns that undergird and integrate. The implication for our worldview is that we are already interconnected.

Speaking of our interconnection as humans, Einstein, in a letter written in 1950, said it this way:

> A human being is part of a whole, called by us the "Universe," a part limited in time and space. He experiences himself, his thoughts and feelings, as something separated from the rest—a kind of optical delusion of his consciousness. The striving to free oneself from this delusion is the one issue of true religion. Not to nourish the delusion but to try to overcome it is the way to reach the attainable measure of peace of mind.[23]

Psychologically and socially, we exist both autonomously and in connection, between independence and interdependence. From the Renaissance to the apex of modernism, we have emphasized the self, our individuality, agency, free will, and the like. This has unleashed incredible creativity and heroic accomplishment, and, of course, it has a downside too: greed and selfishness are part of the option for a life that we get to choose.

But the emerging worldview that emphasizes our life together provides metaphors and recognition that reinforce inherent connections with one another, the world, and ourselves.

The realization of so many of our great models was that we do not just interact but instead we interconnect, interdepend, and thus are interresponsible. Thich Nhat Hanh's term is *interbeing*.[24] This is a fundamental change in worldview that has profound implications for our assumptions about living and learning. As a trend in today's culture, scientist and organizational development expert Peter Senge recognizes it this way:

> Connectedness is the defining feature of the new worldview—connectedness as an organizing principle of the universe, connectedness between the "outer world" of manifest phenomena and the "inner world" of lived experience, and, ultimately connectedness among people and between humans and the larger world. While philosophers and spiritual teachers have long spoken about connectedness, a scientific worldview of connectedness could have sweeping influence in "shifting the whole" given the role of science and technology in the modern world.[25]

From computing and biology to physics and neuroscience, we are increasingly describing how the world works with words like *networks, webs, fields,* and *streams,* instead of simply individual *parts, bits,* and *components,* reduced to their lowest independent nature. The forward edge of technology, for example, is not merely bigger computers: it is better networking—ways of tapping into webs of information. In physics, field theories explain the subatomic world (e.g., nonlocal influence and electromagnetism) in a more satisfactory way than Newton's description. Theoretical physicist Michio Kaku captures this sense of unified field when he claims, "The Universe is a symphony of vibrating strings."[26] Physicist Erwin Schrödinger concluded, "Mind by its very nature is a *singular tetantum*. I should say: the overall number of minds is just one."[27] In biology, interactive field[28] and systems theories[29] are more complete than atomistic "component" explanations for understanding the mechanisms of biological organisms, from the cellular to the social level.

The mind has been contained inside the skull in conventional materialistic accounts, indistinguishable from the physical brain. But the latest understanding helps us see that even our brains functionally interconnect with others. The flourishing field of brain science tells us we operate as a neural web, one that even networks with others, underlying our interconnection in the field of consciousness. This has come to be understood as a neurological reality through the emerging field of *social neuroscience*.[30]

When two violins are located in the same room and a string is plucked on the first one, the string tuned to the same frequency on the second violin will vibrate, thus sounding the note. In the field of acoustics, this is called *sympathetic resonance*. A similar phenomenon occurs between you and me. Lovers, parents, close friends, a good therapist, or a child with her puppy can recognize a kind of emotional resonance as we "feel into" the other or pick up their "vibes" or get "in sync" with them. Through this resonance, we have the capacity to know the other with profound immediacy and directness and in so doing come in touch with their pain, anger, or joy very quickly.

Neuroscience is uncovering a bit of the hardwiring for this linking between mammals. *Mirror neurons* are capable of responding instantaneously to the emotions or actions of another person in such a way that the brain of someone witnessing another person is activated as if they were acting like the person they were seeing. This phenomenon was first identified neurobiologically in macaque monkeys.[31] A monkey was hooked up to an electroencephalogram (EEG) measuring brain electrical activity. At one point, researchers recorded patterns of brain activity when the monkey peeled a banana. But what was most unexpected was that when another monkey or a person peeled a banana in front of the wired-up monkey, the same areas of the brain were activated as if the hooked-up monkey was peeling it himself. It was not just that he was seeing it with corresponding activation of the visual cortex, it was as if he was doing it. This led to the idea of "mirror neurons," constellations of brain tissue that mirror or oscillate with another person's (or monkey's) brain and appear to be a component of empathy. This neurological looping or linking demonstrates a kind of very real connection between minds.

So, if the mind and the universe are indeed webs and networks, fields and streams, intertwined with one another in a dynamic system, then developing the mind is served not by merely *filling us up* with more information—the typical goal of contemporary education—but it is especially about *opening us up* to this inherent interconnection, that is, cultivating the capacities to connect. This is just what the empathic mind does. The integration of this knowing involves refining the balance between objectivity and intimacy, as McClintock and Goodall demonstrate so well.

CHARACTER

From worldwide wars to nuclear arsenals, the violence and technology of the twentieth century has helped underline the point that knowledge without heart and wisdom is dangerous and destructive. Martin Luther King Jr. said it this way:

> [Materialism] leads inevitably to a dead-end street in an intellectually sense-less world. . . . Science can give us only physical power, which if not con-trolled by spiritual power, will lead inevitably to cosmic doom. . . . The old evils continue and the age of reason has been transformed into an age of terror. Selfishness and hatred have not vanished with an enlargement of our educa-tional system and an extension of our legislative policies.[32]

By whatever name—ethics, morality, virtue, values, spirituality, or civil-ity—schools have increasingly been at least implicitly tasked with develop-ing these inner qualities of character. The contemporary backdrop of vio-lence, greed, narcissism, and everything from basic disrespect to poor man-ners invigorates the case for character development as being a legitimate part of public education. We all want students to be contributing community members who use knowledge well and wisely and who can at least get along with others.

But from what center do we teach character? King's statement above suggests that some key principles of the culture are a "dead-end" and have even led to an "age of terror." King's proposition gains support when we look at broadcasts of the unthinkable horrors perpetrated in our world and even in our schools.

Recognizing that there is an array of contributing factors to character failure ranging from poverty to abuse, the emphasis here is that the most insidious sources of violence are ideologies of objectivism and materialism, which treat the other (person, object, the natural world, or even some dis-owned part of self) as an object to possess, use, control, or rid ourselves of.

Such "non-relational" knowing creates environments that lead to a basic sense of insecurity and isolation. Without a solid relational ground and basic sense of trust and security, basic anxiety develops and is manifest in person-ality strategies that include "moving against," "moving away," or "moving toward" others.[33] Much of our social concern these days involves the level of violence, the "moving against" another; much of our educational concern involves the "moving away," the isolation and numbness that stares back at us or simply drops out altogether. The "moving toward" implies dependence and lack of autonomy and individuation. The modernist milieu of objectifica-tion of the other, including the natural world (environment and body), con-tributes to these early experiences and to later ethical and educational fail-ures. We never experience the other's subjectivity; the other remains merely an object for our consumer scrutiny and, thus, alienation and violence are more easily perpetrated.

On the other hand, the empathic mind moves us, in the words of Thomas Berry, from experiencing the universe as a collection of objects to a communion of subjects.[34] An ethic of care emerges organically from such communion.

Because of the profound importance of this kind of knowing, empathy has been described as the basis of moral development[35] and even the trait that makes us most human.[36] We realize our humanity and our divinity through the quality of our meetings. As Martin Buber tells us, "All real living is meeting."[37] When we really meet and understand others, it becomes much more difficult to perpetrate violence against them. This is the root of a living morality.

In her concern for rising levels of aggression, Mary Gordon took the unlikely step of bringing babies and mothers into public school classrooms.[38] In the Roots of Empathy program, a mother and her new baby are brought into a classroom for twenty-seven visits over a school year. An instructor from the program accompanies them and coaches the students to observe the baby's development and label the baby's feelings throughout the visit. The instructor also invites students to notice and reflect upon their own and one another's feelings along the way. Mary relays the story of Darren:

> Daren was the oldest child I ever saw in a Roots of Empathy class. He was in grade 8 and had been held back twice. He was two years older than everyone else and already starting to grow a beard. I knew his story: His mother had been murdered in front of his eyes when he was four years old, and [he] had lived in a succession of foster homes ever since. Darren looked menacing because he wanted us to know he was tough; his head was shaved except for a ponytail at the top and he had a tattoo on the back of his head.

The instructor of the Roots of Empathy program was explaining to the class about the differences in temperament that day. She invited the young mother who was visiting the class with Evan, her six-month-old baby, to share her thoughts about her baby's temperament. Joining in the discussion, the mother told the class how Evan liked to face outward when he was in the Snugli and didn't want to cuddle into her, how she would have preferred to have a "more cuddly" baby. As the class ended, the mother asked if anyone wanted to try on the Snugli, which was green and trimmed with pink brocade. To everyone's surprise Darren offered and as the other students scrambled to get ready for lunch, he strapped it on. Then he asked if he could put Evan in. The mother was a little apprehensive, but she handed him the baby, and he put Evan in, facing toward his chest. Much to the surprise of his mother, the baby snuggled right in and Darren took him to a quiet corner and rocked back and forth with the baby in his arms for several minutes. Finally, he came back to where the mother and Roots of Empathy instructor were waiting and he asked: "If nobody has ever loved you, do you think you could still be a good father?"[39]

When systems link, whether within us or between us, such as Darren and the baby, we find harmony. When we fail to harmonize and integrate, living systems—from individuals to families to countries—tend to move toward either chaos or rigidity.[40]

Notice what the instructor asked: What do you think the baby is feeling? What are you feeling? These simple questions help do two interrelated things essential for opening the empathic mind. The first invites us to take another's perspective—What is the baby feeling? The second recognizes that this kind of knowing is not just an abstract idea but also a felt experience. This movement of knowing from outside to inside, from conceptual to visceral, makes this more intimate, participative, and consistent with our latest understanding of empathic consciousness.

Being able to compare our perceptions with others allows us to open the possibility of multiple points of view and refines our own empathic knowing: "Oh, yeah now that you mention it I did feel that, I just didn't think anything of it until you said it. I need to trust that more." Or, "I never thought of seeing it that way." These simple directions to notice the other and notice inwardly begin to expand empathic capacity and could easily be used in any classroom situation where we are imagining anyone's perspective: "How would you feel, what would you think, how would you see the world if you were the terrorist, that historic figure, a new mother, a crying child?"

I SEE YOU

Educator Linda Lantieri tells about a greeting from Natale in South Africa. Instead of *Hello* or something similar, the word used is *Sawabona*. It translates as "I see you." This simple acknowledgment has profound lessons for our lives.

In an age filled with disconnection, alienation, confusion, search for identity and for belonging, we need to be seen, to be met and understood. In our earliest years we know that being seen by our primary caregivers is essential for our sense of security and impacts development in profound ways. When our caregivers are able to link up with us, read our moods, and respond to our needs, we develop a secure sense of attachment, which is tied to nine key capacities: 1) regulation of the body, especially balancing the parasympathetic nervous system, which helps us settle down; 2) attuned communication; 3) emotional balance (not too little and not too much feeling); 4) fear modulation; 5) response flexibility (essentially this means being able to pause and ponder for a moment before responding); 6) insight; 7) empathy; 8) morality; and 9) attuning to our own flow of felt sense.[41] Together these affect how and how well we navigate in the world, including school.

But what if our rooting is not so ideal? Can we still move toward this high end of integration and flourishing? It turns out that the same fundamental process of attunement between individuals works throughout our life. Whatever our age, whether in our family or with a friend, with a therapist or a boss, and especially a teacher, when we have someone who can read us and respond appropriately, we feel seen, cared for; we belong.

By the way, in addition to others seeing us, these same nine capacities are catalyzed when we tune into ourselves. That is, as explored in the chapter on the contemplative mind, by attuning to our own states of body and mind we grow these abilities to know and balance ourselves.

In a very real sense, any of us—students, educators, parents—are brought into existence when we are seen, acknowledged, understood, and appreciated for who we are. The response to that South African greeting of *Sawabona* is *Shikoba,* which means "I am here." When you see me, you bring me into existence. You help me to show up.

Sometimes at the beginning of class I will ask my students to simply find a nearest partner and take just a few minutes to take turns sharing where they are right now. The listener may reflect back what they hear, ask clarifying questions, offer their attention and empathy but avoid any advice giving. This serves as: 1) a way of practicing empathic listening, 2) a way to make contact with another toward the end of growing a sense of community, and 3) an act of confiding, which is a powerful force for physical and psychological well-being,[42] it usually has the effect of helping us relax and freeing our awareness for the learning task at hand.

In other moments we can ask students to listen deeply. Specifically, the instructions are for the speaker to speak their stream of consciousness on something they are willing to share about themselves. An agreement of confidentiality is first secured all around. The listener is not to offer any verbal response whatsoever but to do their best to just listen deeply with their full attention but without any requirement to respond beyond a nod or facial response. They are simply to try to take in what the other offers and listen deeply. Students regularly report this as especially powerful on both sides—listener and speaker—as they are freed to simply flow with their thoughts as the speaker and simply receive the other as the listener without having to figure out what to say.

In one project, teachers enrolled in a graduate education course taught by professor Tom Peterson were invited to try "to see" a difficult student. Specifically, the assignment was to connect with a student whom they saw as especially disconnected. In response, most chose low or underachieving students who were particularly challenging and often frustrating in some way. This intentional relationship may begin with the teacher explaining that they too are a student and they have an assignment to interview someone. The contact might begin by asking a simple question such as, "Please tell me about something you like."

As part of his assignment for this project, instead of simply disciplining him yet once again, Lawrence decided to sit down with seventeen-year-old TJ, who is described by his teacher as "a loud, cocky, and obnoxious seventeen-year-old who I would regularly have to reprimand and remove from class. He had a way of just getting under my skin." On this day after a typical disruption Lawrence pulled TJ aside and sat down to talk. He asked, "What can I do to help you and what can you do to help me?" Lawrence noted, "I did not think any real progress was made but the next week I did notice that he was a little quieter in class and actually brought his book and a notebook to class." The following week, TJ asked whether, if he remained quiet, he could draw a picture in response to a group project that required students to read and answer questions about their lesson on the Middle Ages. Lawrence agreed, and it turned out that this unruly student communicated with clarity and virtuosity through his impressive artwork. TJ ended up drawing a creative and accurate solution to the question posed.

In a subsequent conversation, Lawrence asked TJ to describe the most important person in his life. TJ spent several animated minutes describing his young brother. "He even said that keeping his brother safe and cared for is 'my only goal in life.' I asked him why he felt this way. 'My brother is the only one who loves me just the way I am. [My mother] loves me because I bring home [money]. My grandma loves me because I help pay the bills. Tommy, he just loves me because he wants to.'" In Lawrence's eyes, this hardened and "obnoxious" individual became a tender brother. His teacher began to see him for the first time.

Kelly, an eighteen-year-old tenth-grader, did not attend school regularly, and when she did come, she laid her head on the desk, covered her head with a coat, and went to sleep. After a few brief "interviews" conducted after school in which her teacher simply tried to invite conversation and ask about Kelly's life and interests, her teacher said, "I noticed that Kelly began to take more of an interest in her studies. She started listening in class. She didn't go to sleep. She participated in class activities and discussion. When the six-week report cards were issued, she was passing all of her subjects for the first time. I feel differently about her. I have more compassion and a genuine affection toward Kelly."

Six-year-old David never spoke to or interacted with other children. He walked into class with his head down and responded to the good morning greeting (and nearly every other comment) with "I hate school." Terry, his speech teacher, decided that she would place David in a small group for their twice-weekly meetings. She also decided to pick David up personally from his classroom. "I made an extra effort to reach out to him in the hallways, as he was getting on the bus, and in our sessions. By the end of April, he began shyly waving and saying, in the lowest voice possible, 'Hi, Miss Davis.' He began eagerly wanting to do activities in class. He began interacting with the two other boys in his group. He began talking with them, asking them questions, even arguing with them."

Mary describes her experience with Jane, a hearing-impaired student from a family of ten children living in a federal housing project. Mary had attempted to make an effort to communicate with Jane (who seemed entirely isolated) first by speaking through her signing interpreter and then by learning some sign language herself. "Jane, who never communicated with anyone in class, started to come to my homeroom before the other students and talk to me about her family and her school work. She acted very shy in class around other students in the beginning, but as she and I began to communicate more she became more involved with the other students. One day, after we had been meeting for a few weeks she came into school quite upset and I learned that she was menstruating for the first time and had been unprepared for this by her mother. She was very fearful and upset. We talked about it and I assured her that it was normal and that everything would be fine. I hugged her. When she left she said, 'I love you. Thank you for caring about me.' When she left my room, tears rolled down my cheeks and I felt very happy to have had the opportunity to know this child. I felt a sensation of love vibrate through my body."

We know that these relationships are not magical cures; students may fall back into a disconnected life, one overwhelmed by poverty and violence, conflict and alienation, disappointment and dispossession. Students drop out. TJ says, "I can't quit work [forty hours a week] to go to school regularly or my little brother Tommy won't eat regular. Martha [his disabled mother] doesn't get enough money to support us on her own." Cultures like TJ's affect us to our bones, but often one real and dependable contact, a "leg-up" person, may be sufficient to catalyze success and resilience. The resilient child almost invariably has someone who sees and understands him or her.

While we may have an impulse to scoop up a poverty-stricken child, or to make a project out of saving a social outcast, the point of meeting is not to rescue but to understand—to care, not to cure. Understanding or empathy implies knowing and may stimulate an impulse for mercy or service, but the center of what it does is to open our heart. This helps us avoid molding the student into what we think the student should be. Simply from this meeting, both lives may be changed.

As significant as the change in students can be (better attitude, cooperation, performance, social engagement), the change that the teacher describes in himself or herself is just as noteworthy. Mary says, "I began to develop closer and more meaningful relationships with my students as a result of this experience and I see students in a different light. I have also learned to be more patient with my own daughter."

Katherine says, "This experience changed me more than it did [the student]." Teresa, who interviewed a sixteen-year-old, dispossessed, "counterculture" girl, reports, "After being around Ann I realize that maybe I only take time with the 'good' kids, the students that seemed more like I was in school. I now wonder how many Anns there are in my classes. How many children just want one person to ask them a question about themselves?" Terry, who met with six-year-old David, says, "I realize that I am in a position to change lives. On the other hand, I am in a position to have my life changed." Lawrence says, "I can never go into a classroom again without seeing TJ in the faces of each of my students. Each will have a story to tell from now on. When you start to see students as people with real needs beyond the sphere of typical education it becomes very difficult to stay focused on the task at hand. I felt that it was my responsibility to stay within the guidelines and focus on how I could help them through the curriculum. Now I have to rethink that position. The boundaries have become fuzzy and the zones of black and white have become gray. Maybe I am learning what good teaching and the truth really are."[43]

When the heart opens, boundaries do grow fuzzy. No longer are we left with subject versus object, task versus relationship, but we see through the eye of the heart. As already mentioned, an understanding relationship not only develops the "soft" noncurricular areas (social skills, feelings of connectedness); these are also directly bound to how we behave and perform in school. Our self-discipline, motivation, attention, and performance are tied to this relational domain. If we want to improve performance, especially among the most difficult students, then understanding and relationship are essential.

We are social beings, hardwired to connect with one another. We are coming to understand that in a very real, in-the-world sense, social intelligence is more important than knowing chemistry, for example. Social neuroscientist Matthew Lieberman, among others, argues that the human brain has evolved to be social and has done so because there are profound advantages to understanding others. Those bonds we feel toward others help us empathize, "increase[ing] our capacity to predict what is going on in the minds of others so we can better coordinate and cooperate with them."[44] We have a need to belong, to connect, to be seen and understood. If our sense of connection and belonging is frayed, we are not as available to learn.

In one study examining the effect of social rejection on intellectual performance, individuals in the experimental group were told essentially that in the future they were more likely to be alone than other people. Researchers were trying to manipulate participants' feeling of disconnection. Participants then took either an IQ test or a GRE-style test. The results: in the GRE-type test participants in the control group got 68 percent correct while the rejected group got only 39 percent. In the IQ test: 82 percent correct for the control versus 69 percent for the rejected group.[45] Belonging makes a difference not only in how we feel but even in how we perform.

SERVICE AS KNOWING

One very direct way to experiment with empathy and understanding is through service. Service is important not just to fill the needs of the culture, or because it is the moral or good thing to do, but because it actually opens our consciousness, our ways of knowing.[46]

When a child takes the classroom turtle home for the weekend, it is primarily a lesson in service and responsibility to the turtle and to the class. When young children have plants to care for they are learning the lessons of service to the community of nature. When an older student helps a younger one, a bond is usually formed as the two come into relationship with one another and with the material at hand. A sense of pleasure and pride in the accomplishments of one another often emerges if the relationship takes root. This relationship develops between students of any age. Sixth-graders help out in kindergarten; eleventh-graders help with eighth-grade math; university students volunteer as tutors throughout the primary and secondary grades. Peer tutoring provides an opportunity for connection and collaboration, not only taking advantage of expertise, but also tapping the power of social interest we have especially at middle school and beyond.

Our minds are so geared toward the social exchange that it is not only in the act of helping but even in thinking that we will be helping or teaching that enhances learning. In a series of studies, thinking that we are going to teach someone else about the material, even if we never teach them, improves learning.[47] Learning-for-teaching provides a social motivation and practical relevance that helps us understand well enough so that we can share with another.

When a dove got out of its cage in class, Megan, his elementary teacher, spontaneously gave seven-year-old Kendrick, whom she described as "extremely disruptive and uninterested," the responsibility to capture, hold, and care for the dove before placing it back in the cage. She did not really have a plan or know how this would go, but there he was and there the bird was and in that instant she asked. He responded immediately and gently and carefully went to collect the feathery escapee. She says, "When another student came up to my desk and tried to help he politely told them it was his job and he could finish it on his own. He had rarely spoken politely to adults before that moment, much less to his classmates. For the first time I saw a caring side of [him]. Up to that point, when I had tried to hug him, he would freeze up, as if he did not know what to do. Now we can't get him to stop giving us hugs. At the end of the next day he approached me and said that he wanted to come

back to school the next day. Previously he would only say: 'I hate school.'"
She goes on to say that not only was he much more pleasant to be around but
also his school performance suddenly exploded. One day in class "when
asked to describe his favorite teacher he wrote, 'Mrs. Partain I like.' I was
amazed to have gotten that much structure since most days I just received a
conglomeration of letters copied at random; often I could not even read them.
Now, he had not only written words that were not displayed on the word list
but had organized them into a phrase to answer the question. A few weeks
later, after some help from a volunteer, he read his first book. I was so proud
of him that I started crying as he was reading to me."

In a residential psychiatric facility called Inner Harbor, middle-grade
boys in a classroom (they attend school at the facility) were each given a
colorful betta fish, also known as a Siamese fighting fish. The boys were
entirely responsible for the care of the fish and through earned credits for
good behavior they could purchase items like a larger bowl and accessories
for the fish's "crib"—a tiny treasure chest, colorful stones, and so forth. The
relationships that emerged were transformative for nearly all of the boys.
Eleven-year-old Justin explained the role he had with his fish, Sparky. "I
have to feed him and take care of him. He depends on me." Some of the
children will speak in therapy about how the fish won't yell or abuse them.
All of the children who were given fish have been extraordinarily attentive
and gentle with their little charges. They have also developed respect and
empathy toward other students as they feel how much their own fish means
to them and imagine the same for the peers. This simple process of connection and care has been a powerful guide for these boys. They parent a fish
with the kind of gentle concern that in many cases they did not receive from
their own parents. But Justin understands that this is a two-way relationship.
"When I feel hyper, I just put my finger on the tank and Sparky looks at me.
It calms me down."

Some among us have seen happiness and service as intertwined, not only
powerful for learning and emotional balance. Mother Theresa understood it
this way:

> To me, God and compassion are one and the same. Compassion is the joy of
> sharing. It's doing the small things for the love of each other—just a smile, or
> carrying a bucket of water, of showing some simple kindness. . . . The fruit of
> love is service, which is compassion in action. [48]

It turns out that the kind of happiness derived from service makes a
difference not only for our learning and relationships, but even at the molecular level. In an age where we all seem to be seeking happiness, some activities take happiness all the way down to our bones, and further.

A bit of pleasure—a piece of cake, for example—however welcome and enjoyable, is somehow different than helping someone in need. This hedonic versus eudaimonic difference, long acknowledged by philosophers, has now found distinction at the molecular level. Psychology professor Barbara Fredrickson and colleagues have uncovered different patterns of gene expression within immune cells resulting from different kinds of pleasure.

We know that stress causes a pattern of gene expression involved in inflammation. Inflammation in the body has been implicated in everything from heart disease to arthritis. But it turns out that eudaimonic activity— genuine service—actually results in a decrease in inflammation response at the cellular level. By contrast, hedonic pleasures result in an increase in inflammation. When we care for another being, it looks like we also end up taking care of our own well-being.[49]

The growth of culture, classrooms, and consciousness depends on a way of knowing that somehow integrates the heart. A more intimate, relational way of knowing complements the power of objective, critical detachment. This more participative knowing is consistent with the emerging worldview of a universe that is interconnected at every level from the molecular to the social. The empathic mind involves an attitude of curiosity and appreciation, a willingness to meet and participate with the other, to feel into and take on another's perspective, to meet rather than simply manipulate. This helps us to see and be seen, to belong and connect. As empathy is closely tied to the development of morality, the empathic mind serves as a foundation of character and an impetus for service and care.

The Jesuit sage and world-class paleontologist Pierre Teilhard de Chardin speaks of this way of knowing as the key to the next leap in our evolution:

> The day will come when, after harnessing the ether, the winds, the waves, the tides, gravitation, we shall harness for God the energies of love. And, on that day, for the second time in the history of the world, man will have discovered fire.[50]

We have arrived at the point in history where our thriving and our surviving depend on this.

NOTES

1. Thomas Berry, *The Great Work: Our Way into the Future* (New York: Random House, 1999), 149.

2. Antoine de Saint-Exupéry, *The Little Prince*, trans. Richard Howard (New York: Harcourt, 2000), 63; original work published 1943.

3. Erwin Schrodinger, *What Is Life? Mind and Matter* (London: Cambridge University Press, 1945), 140.

4. Parker Palmer, *To Know as We Are Known: Education as a Spiritual Journey* (San Francisco: HarperSanFrancisco, 1993), 23.

5. William James, *A Pluralistic Universe* (Cambridge, MA: Harvard University Press, 1977), 19; original work published 1909.

6. Sy Montgomery, *Walking with the Great Apes: Jane Goodall, Dian Fossey, Birute Galdikas* (New York: Houghton Mifflin, 1991), 128.

7. Ibid., 261.

8. Jane Goodall with Phillip Berman, *Reason for Hope: A Spiritual Journey* (New York: Grand Central Publishing, 2000), 78.

9. Martin Buber, *I and Thou*, trans. R. G. Smith (New York: Charles Scribner & Sons, 1958); original work published 1923.

10. Thich Nhat Hanh, *The Miracle of Mindfulness* (Boston: Beacon Press, 1975), 61.

11. Martin Heidegger, "What Calls for Thinking?," in *Basic Writings,* ed. D. F. Krell (New York: HarperCollins, 1993), 365–391; original work published 1977.

12. Buber, *I and Thou.*

13. Evelyn Fox Keller, *A Feeling for the Organism: The Life and Work of Barbara McClintock* (New York: Henry Holt, 1983), 198.

14. Abraham Heschel, *God in Search of Man* (New York: Octagon Books, 1972), 78; original work published 1955.

15. Ibid., 46.

16. Ruth Shlossman, "Can You Teach Empathy?," *Tikkun 11*, no. 2 (1996): 20.

17. David Hamilton, Lawrence Katz, and Von O. Leirer, "Cognitive Representation of Personality Impression: Organizational Processes in First Impression Formation," *Journal of Personality and Social Psychology* 39, no. 6 (1980): 1050.

18. Matthew D. Lieberman, *Social: Why Our Brains Are Wired to Connect* (New York: Crown, 2013), 286–288.

19. Parts of this section are also published in Tobin Hart, *The Four Virtues: Presence, Heart, Wisdom, Creation* (New York: Atria, 2014).

20. David Bohm, *Wholeness and the Implicate Order* (Boston: Routledge & Kegan Paul, 1980).

21. Ibid., 172.

22. Gregory Bateson, *Mind and Nature: A Necessary Unity* (New York: Bantam Books, 1980).

23. Albert Einstein to Robert S. Marcus, 12 February 1950, Albert Einstein Archives, The Hebrew University of Jerusalem, Israel.

24. Thich Nhat Hanh, *The Heart of Understanding: Commentaries on the Prajna-paramita Heart Sutra* (Berkeley: Parallax Press, 1995).

25. Peter Senge, Otto Scharmer, Joseph Jaworski, and Betty Sue Flowers, *Presence: An Exploration of Profound Change in People, Organizations, and Society* (New York: Doubleday, 2005), 188.

26. Michio Kaku, "What Happened Before the Big Bang?," *Astronomy* 24, no. 5 (1996).

27. Erwin Schrödinger, *What Is Life? With Mind and Matter and Autobiographical Sketches* (London: Cambridge University Press, 1945).

28. For example, Rupert Sheldrake, *The Presence of the Past: Morphic Resonance and the Habits of Nature* (South Paris, ME: Park Street Press, 1995).

29. For example, Ludwig von Bertalanffy, *General System Theory: Foundations, Development, Applications* (New York: George Braziller, 1968).

30. For example, Daniel Goleman, *Social Intelligence: The New Science of Human Relationships* (New York: Random House, 2006); and Daniel Siegel, *The Developing Mind: How Relationships and the Brain Interact to Shape Who We Are* (New York: Guilford Press, 1999).

31. Ferdinand Binkofski and Giovanni Buccino, "Therapeutic Reflection," *Scientific American Mind* 18, no. 3 (2007): 78–81.

32. Martin Luther King Jr., *Strength to Love* (New York: Harper & Row, 1963), 55, 56, 120.

33. Karen Horney, *Neurosis and Human Growth: The Struggle Toward Self-Realization* (New York: W. W. Norton, 1950).

34. Berry, *The Great Work*, 16.

35. Martin L. Hoffman, "Empathy and Justice Motivation," *Motivation and Emotion* 14, no. 2 (1990): 151–172.

36. Beth Azar, "Defining the Trait that Makes Us Most Human," *APA Monitor* 28, no. 11 (1997): 1–15.

37. Buber, *I and Thou*, 11.

38. Mary Gordon, *Roots of Empathy: Changing the World Child by Child* (Toronto, CA: Thomas Allen, 2005).

39. Ibid., 6.

40. Daniel J. Seigel, *Mindsight: The New Science of Personal Transformation* (New York: Bantam, 2010).

41. Daniel J. Siegel, *The Developing Mind: How Our Relationships and the Brain Interact to Shape Who We Are* (New York: Aldine, 1999).

42. See, for example, James W. Pennebaker, J. K. Kiecolt-Glasser, and R. Glasser, "Disclosure of Trauma and Immune Functioning: Health Implications for Psychotherapy," *Journal of Consulting and Clinical Psychology* 56, no. 2 (1988): 239–245; and S. P. Spera, E. D. Buhrfeind, and James W. Pennebaker, "Expressive Writing and Coping With Job Loss," *Academy of Management Journal* 37 (1994): 722–733.

43. Tobin Hart, *From Information to Transformation: Education for the Evolution of Consciousness* (New York: Peter Lang, 2009).

44. Lieberman, *Social,* 9.

45. Roy Baumeister, Jean Twenge, and Christopher Nuss, "Effects of Social Exclusion on Cognitive Processes: Anticipated Loneliness Reduces Intelligent Thought," *Journal of Personality and Social Psychology* 83, no. 4 (2002): 817.

46. See Arthur Deikman, "Service as Knowing," in *Transpersonal Knowing: Exploring the Horizon of Consciousness,* eds. Tobin Hart, Peter Nelson, and Kaisa Puhakka (Albany, NY: State University of New York Press, 2000), 303–318.

47. John A. Bargh and Yaacov Schul, "On the Cognitive Benefits of Teaching," *Journal of Educational Psychology* 72, no. 5 (1980): 593.

48. Mother Teresa, *For the Love of God: New Writings by Spiritual and Psychological Leaders*, eds. B. Shield and R. Carlson (San Rafael, CA: New World Library, 1990), 151.

49. Barbara L. Fredrickson et al., "A Functional Genomic Perspective on Human Well-Being," *Proceedings of the National Academy of Sciences of the United States of America* 110, no. 33 (August 2013): 13684–13689, doi: 10.1073/pnas.1305419110; University of North Carolina at Chapel Hill, "Human Cells Respond in Healthy, Unhealthy Ways to Different Kinds of Happiness," *ScienceDaily* (July 2013) http://www.sciencedaily.com/releases/2013/07/130729161952.htm.

50. Pierre Teilhard De Chardin, *Toward the Future,* trans. R. Hague (New York: Harcourt Brace Jovanovich, 1975), 86–87; original work published 1973.

Chapter Three

Beautiful Mind

Beauty will save the world.

—Fyodor Dostoyevsky [1]

The ancients knew that somehow value and virtue in life is not only about the good and the true, it is also beautiful. Through beauty we recognize qualities that make one thing more inviting or valuable than another: this provides meaning and a kind of magnetism. We cannot necessarily measure it precisely or even explain it and therefore it has been more difficult to incorporate into industrial-era curricula. But somehow beauty sends a "ping" into our own depths.

The attention to beauty is so culturally and historically ubiquitous that it is surely natural to our human existence. In human culture beauty shows up all over the place, including in two important bookends of making sense of our existence: religion and evolution. Taking a moment to notice how beauty finds its way into these two realms helps to demonstrate just how central and significant it is.

Religion has been a way of capturing what is of highest value in human existence. Every religious tradition creates beauty to express or honor what is understood as most sacred. Creating beauty has been both an act of devotion, an outpouring expressing our connection and commitment, and an act of invocation, used to move us into a state of reverence. From European cathedrals to Islamic mosques, from gospel hymns to Hindu chants, from Russian iconography to Tibetan sand paintings, beauty is offered as a gift and a prayer to what is most sacred to us. It is a testament to the importance we place on the sacred, but equally it testifies to how dear we hold beauty.

Beauty of a different sort shapes another way we think about creation: the process of evolution. Beauty befuddled Darwin, who understood that adaptations that favored stronger or more effective design of creatures would win the day and enable them to pass their genes along—natural selection. But he discovered something else: "The sight of a feather in a peacock's tail, whenever I gaze at it, makes me sick!"[2] Evolution was not only practical, for some reason it liked a kind of beauty. In time he came to understand that natural selection had a mate in sexual selection. And sexual selection favored attributes that seemed aesthetically interesting—like the male peacock's feathers, or the male baboon's rump, or the redness of the dot on a bird's beak. Evolution, so it seems, favors beauty.

"Beauty will save the world," writes Russian novelist Fyodor Dostoyevsky in *The Idiot*. Philosopher Alfred North Whitehead says the teleology of the universe is the production of beauty.[3] Helen of Troy was said to have a face so beautiful that it launched a thousand ships. Even the chairman of General Motors, an industrial-era (think function, efficiency, sort of) icon, said that his company's job was to produce "moving sculpture." This behemoth of the machine age defined its work as art. In fact, manufacturing has made a turn toward beauty. Some cars are for transportation, and others are to die for. Apple has made products that are aesthetically pleasing in form and function, to its great success. We can now buy toilet bowl brushes with attention to more than the stiffness of their bristles. Industrial design and marketing recognizes the value in beauty, but education has yet to realize that beauty has "cred" not only on the street and in the marketplace but especially in the human mind.

Beauty is more than ornamentation. There is something in beauty that touches our common humanity. We hunger for beauty; in and of itself beauty is nourishment and a necessity. We recognize it, we talk of it, yet it remains difficult to define—we might call it "quality." We live according to an intuitive sense of its meaning, and when we stay true to it, it guides most of our attitudes and decisions.

It is not simply the surface that makes the beautiful. Sometimes we confuse the shell for the nut. But instead beauty reflects some underlying quality that is revealed when form and perception meet and open to one another. In the beautiful object or act we see what we want to join with. C. S. Lewis said it this way:

> We do not want merely to see beauty. . . . We want something else that can hardly be put into words—to be united with the beauty we see, to pass into it, to receive it into ourselves, to bathe in it, to become part of it.[4]

In the third century Plotinus made sense of the strange gravitational pull of beauty in this way. He said that our earthly embodiment means that you and I are splintered from the divine. Our soul carries that imprint, and in beauty we get a glimpse of that divinity, our true home base. We sense perfection of that other world, and the soul strives to reunite with it.

Said in a more contemporary way, we are hardwired for beauty. That ping, that magnetism, connects to something both deep within us and beyond us. When we see yellow, it is not just out there; it resonates and is recognized inside. Beauty brings knower and knowledge closer to one another, one of the fundamental directions of the integrative mind.

BEAUTY IN UNEXPECTED PLACES

While it is not hard to recognize the role of beauty in the arts and humanities—the arc of a dancer or the rhythm of a poem—it is more surprising that even the supposed detachment and objectivity of science seems to have beauty entwined in its roots.

Modernism split science from the arts. But the differences between them were turned into artificial division, as if they had nothing to do with one another and no way to relate.

In education the result of this gulf limits the growth of the mind. William Lipscomb concludes, "If one actually set out to give as little help as possible to both aesthetics and originality in science, one could hardly devise a better plan than our educational system. . . . One rarely hears about what we do not understand in science, and least of all how to prepare for creative ideas."[5]

Bridging the gulf between science and beauty, Robert Augros and George Stanciu in *The New Story of Science* show us that incredibly "all of the most eminent physicists of the twentieth century agree that beauty is the primary standard for scientific truth."[6] French mathematician and theoretical physicist Henri Poincaré understood the role of beauty in science in this way:

> The scientist does not study nature because it is useful to do so. He studies it because he takes pleasure in it; and he takes pleasure in it because it is beautiful. If nature were not beautiful, it would not be worth knowing and life would not be worth living. . . . I mean the intimate beauty which comes from the harmonious order of its parts and which a pure intelligence can grasp.[7]

Plato understood that one kind of beauty comes through the universality of the logic of mathematics. For Plato it is particularly the qualities—harmony, balance, and proportion—within the object or act that we love, not the objects themselves. Here is Plato's description of the beauty of architecture:

> What I understand here by beauty . . . is not what the common man generally understands by this term, as for example the beauty of living things and their representation. On the contrary, it is sometimes rectilinear . . . and circular, with the surfaces of solid bodies composed by means of compasses, the chord,

the setsquare. For these forms are not like others, beautiful under certain conditions; they are always beautiful in themselves. [8]

Mathematician Steven Strogatz finds beauty and wonder akin to Plato's in the discovery of a hidden universe during a schoolroom lesson:

> Our teacher handed us a little toy pendulum that was retractable, that is you could change the links of the string like an old telescope. *Click, click, click.* Then the teacher gave us a stopwatch and said, "I want you to time how long it takes for this pendulum to swing back and forth 10 times." So I do the experiment. *Ten swings . . . click.* I record how many seconds it took and then I write that in my little freshman lab notebook.
>
> Well, then he says now make the pendulum a little bit longer, one click longer, *click.* I do it again. It takes longer to make the ten swings and I write down the number, and I do this five or six times dutifully plotting the results on graph paper which is what the experiment was really supposed to teach us—how to use graph paper. But what it taught me was this spooky thing was happening which is that the dots were falling on an arc, on a curve. They weren't in a straight line; they were on a particular curve. I noticed that this curve was a curve I had seen before because I had just learned about it in algebra class and it's called a parabola. And this really gave me the creeps. I had this sort of feeling of hairs standing on the back of my neck because it was as if this inanimate thing, this pendulum knew algebra. And my thirteen-year-old mind couldn't understand that. How could this thing swinging back and forth know something about parabolas? It was in that moment that I suddenly understood what people mean when they say there's a law of nature.
>
> There was this sort of veil over reality, a hidden universe that you couldn't see unless you knew math. It really felt like being let into some sort of secret society. And that wasn't so much the point. I mean, it's not like I cared about being in this priesthood. It's a very intimate personal thing, this feeling of wonder of a sense of living in an incomprehensible and beautiful universe. But partly comprehensible, that's the beauty of it. [9]

Great scientists and discoverers of all sorts regularly express the passion and beauty for their work and for the world. They tap deeply into the nature of nature, or whatever they are exploring. There is often a profound sense of awe, wonder, and beauty that is expressed, and this provides a kind of reverential attitude toward the cosmos. It seems to be an almost natural outcome of this deep meeting.

I recall the feeling of mystery and intrigue each time I entered Mr. Simpson's sixth-grade science class. He was an environmentalist and naturalist well ahead of his time, at least in my little rural town. I would see this tall, respectable-looking man walk home from school and pick up all the trash between his house and the school; he spoke of poison apples (pesticide laden) and the particularities of the coloring on birds; he developed a nature trail behind the school. His room always seemed to have layers and layers of fascinating, real stuff, from a wasp's nest to a human skeleton, to rocks and minerals.

One time when a couple of us had to make a delivery of some sort to his house, his wife directed us behind the house in order to find him in his small, one-room workshop that was nestled among large trees and untamed bushes. We did not expect what we would find. Filling up the small space were scores of woodcarvings of birds. They were incredibly detailed, at various stages of being shaped, smoothed, and painted. We were instantly stilled, somehow expecting them to fly off if we moved too quickly. I remember being struck at how beautiful, detailed, and (this is the best word I can find) tender his birds were. His keen eye and skilled hand captured some quality that seemed really remarkable. We were suddenly let into a secret garden, so it seemed, and into a way of meeting the world that was deeply important and tender like these birds.

While I had some interest in science and the natural word, it was Mr. Simpson's fascination and slightly eccentric personality that drew in many of my classmates and me far enough to find what was beautiful. There was mystery and wonder here, not just facts to be picked up. Maybe the most important thing about his pedagogy was that he was still fascinated and did not hide it. He might get "off track" speculating on the development of some rock or imagining the owner of some bone, just "thinking out loud," wondering beneath the surface. Most significantly, this meant that we could be fascinated and wonder too. And amidst the growing concern to avoid social stigmatization and be cool, we did not have to be afraid to show our fascination and look for the beauty.

He entered the mystery with us, led us in really, with a profound appreciation for the beauty of the thing. I suppose he had a curriculum to follow, but he wanted to show us stuff, and have us show him our little found treasures. He helped us to see the world as treasure, as beautiful.

Religionist Abraham Heschel recognized that

> our systems of education stress the importance of enabling the student to exploit the power aspect of reality. . . . We teach the children how to measure, how to weigh. We fail to teach them how to revere, how to sense wonder and awe. [10]

Beauty takes endless forms: a great work of art, a perfect lapis sky, but also a perfect pitch in baseball, a meal prepared with special attention to detail, the deep peace of an infant asleep in loving arms, an act of kindness or courage can be beautiful. We hunger for this. Not just the artist creating a sculpture or the designer arraigning space, but also ourselves giving attention to the way the lawn is mowed or beholding the wonder of a night sky.

We also use the word to speak of an act or an art that somehow embodies both imminence and transcendence all at once. Martin Luther King's "I have a dream" speech was a combination of well-considered craftsmanship and spontaneous riff. He practiced the preacher's art; he had been workshopping and testing various ideas in his speeches until it came together in a profound way on the steps of the Lincoln Memorial that day in 1963. But it was not only the beauty of his prose; it was the transcendent beauty of the ideas, the hope and vision for a greater humanity that was at its root.

Beauty names not just a pretty face or a nice painting. It may also take the form of social justice, wholeness, or transcendence. We are trying to capture something that speaks to excellence, or goodness or realness or maybe that splinter of the divine that Plotinus understood, or those laws of nature or something we cannot quite put our finger on but that we recognize nonetheless as awakening a vital aspect of our consciousness, our humanity, and thus is central to knowing the world deeply.

BEAUTY AND KNOWING

Where does beauty come from in the mind? We will not find a brain part responsible for beauty but we may be able to see something else. While our individual sense of beauty may sometimes be radically variable and individual ("You like this picture; I prefer that one"), the process of knowing that enables beauty may be somewhat more universal. Specifically, the interplay of *harmony* and *intensity* may constitute a dynamic process underlying both learning and beauty. In addition, the quality of knowing that we call *presence* helps to reveal beauty by expanding our awareness of harmony and intensity.

One primary way the mind develops is through an intertwined process of differentiation and integration. We make distinctions and then bring together parts advancing into a new patterned whole. We notice the difference between the sound and meaning of words (e.g., Dad and Dog) or give names to different shades of, say, yellow (sunflower, saffron, butter, banana) and then find a way for them to coexist in our mental map or schema of the world. Beauty is so universal to our existence and so useful for learning because it may be fundamentally tied to this same process of knowing.

Philosopher Alfred North Whitehead argues that beauty emerges out of a process of differentiation or contrast on the one hand and integration or harmony on the other. Light and shadow join with one another to produce a mood and image; various tones merge together and are contrasted with silence or gaps to form rhythm and melody; tension is built and released in a powerful story or a song. Contradictions become contrasts and contrasts elicit depth.[11] And remember that what we are shooting for in an integrative mind is depth. In a state of beauty, the contrast between parts brings everything into focus, so that "the parts contribute to the massive feeling of the whole, and the whole contributes to the intensity of feeling of the parts."[12]

For Whitehead, the challenge of beauty is the dual aim of harmony and intensity, unity in diversity (or integration amidst differentiation). If the contrast is too great, there is a "painful clash" and the result can be a mess.[13] If the inclusion is too limited, the lack of diversity leads to tameness and monotony. Beauty rests on "not only the absence of conflict (harmony), but also the realization of new contrasts (intensity),"[14] and "contrasts of contrasts."[15] In Whitehead's conception, "Contrast is the opposite of incompatibility . . . *to set in contrast with* means *to put in a unity with.*"[16] This is not static but continues to expand as we come to recognize subtler or previously unseen contrasts as well as freshly perceived patterns or integrations.

Anticipating the emergent episteme, Whitehead says that value is achieved from "the vivid grasp of the interdependence of the one and the many."[17] Essentially the whole point of existence, he contends, is the creation of beauty, this fusion of discord and harmony, of parts and wholes, of difference and integration.

If at its heart beauty along with learning has to do with a process of contrast and unity, distinction and harmony, then anytime we engage in these two interrelated dimensions significantly we move toward depth. Asking students to notice distinctions or contrasts of ideas or objects can begin a process of differentiation, whether in distinguishing the constitution of different kinds of clouds, or the spelling of words, or from the perspective of a freedom fighter versus a terrorist. "Compare and contrast" style assignments generally go half way, typically emphasizing the capacity for differentiation. They are useful but often feel unsatisfying and incomplete, an indication that the mind wants more.

The next step is to explore their integration, that is, how these relate to one another and perhaps to a larger whole, whether in the natural world (e.g., global warming, weather patterns, and plankton) or the social world (e.g., the interplay between economics, terrorism, ideology, history, and so forth). These contrasts, from the most rudimentary to complex points of view, set in motion a process that seeks integration, reconciliation, and harmony, and brings depth and intensity to learning, leading to "balanced complexity," synthesizing a wide variety of materials into a harmonious whole.

In a learning situation, we can help students deepen understanding by directing their focus on differentiation and integration. We will use the word "beauty" here, but we could just as easily use other words that capture the particularities of experience, such as: "better or worse," "more or less desirable," "quality," "colder," "fairer," "meaner," and so forth depending on the direction of the lesson. The point is just to draw out contrast and harmony. Here is a handful of the type of directions that may help to do so:

- Experiencing beauty: Think of something that is beautiful (or fair or wise or ugly or whatever might be useful to frame the particular topic) to you. What is your experience, the feeling, thoughts, and sensations that are evoked?
- Quality and discernment: What makes this more beautiful (or better, worse, etc.) than that?
- Identity: When and how has beauty made an impact on you?
- Epistemology: How do you know something is beautiful? What makes it so?
- Values: When is beauty also good or true?
- Classical beauty: Notice harmony, balance, pattern, the golden mean, and such.
- Radical beauty: Notice something that has great intensity but that may not be appreciated by everyone.
- Natural beauty: What do you notice about the natural world and about your experience while in it?
- Transformation and paradox: When does beauty become ugly (e.g., a great athlete does something dastardly—takes a cheap shot)? By what means does something ugly become beautiful?
- Perception: Has something grown more or less beautiful over time through your eyes or others?

Presence

As a unique moment of harmony and intensity, every occasion is to some degree beautiful. I remember dropping a daughter off at swim practice one afternoon. The facility was next to the small manmade lake that sits in our small town. A former student who happened to be visiting rode along so we might squeeze in a little more time to talk. We went for a short walk along the lake, which I sometimes did when waiting for swim practice to end. I had been mentioning something about longing to live on a beautiful lake and must have implied that this one was not as beautiful as I would hope for. She hesitated in our walk and said, "You know, right now this is the most beautiful lake I have ever seen." I knew that she had seen many lakes that we both knew were more gorgeous than this—had a nicer shoreline, clearer water. But I could see that she was dead serious. She was open to beholding the beauty that was in front of her in this moment. I suddenly wondered what I had been shutting out through some judgment, how I had been filtering beauty out rather than taking it in, how I had put this lake in a category rather than meeting it in this moment. I have not passed by that lake since without seeing it in a new light. Sure, I know there is more beautiful water out there, but most days I can see that it *is* beautiful. [18]

Beauty reflects the quality of our knowing as much as it does the object before us.

Beauty may indeed exist outside of the knower—a great work of art or a magnificent tree—but it is comprehended or covered over, enacted or ignored by the human mind and heart. A key to beauty is that we cocreate it through the quality of our presence. As we open awareness—our feelings, thoughts, sensations—to something or someone we can notice beneath the surface.

As we dive in, the world unfolds before us and within us. Like a great naturalist, we begin to see more depth, more subtlety, and, ultimately, more beauty. The opening of awareness and perception can reveal the beauty in all things. William Blake, English poet and mystic, tells us, "If the doors of perception were cleansed, everything would appear to man as it is, infinite. For man has closed himself up, till he sees all things thro' narrow chinks of his cavern."[19]

The beautiful is codependent with presence. There is a difference between racing through an art museum to see if you can see everything and instead *beholding*, almost communing with a work of art. This is a shift from quantity to quality. In a classroom there is always pressure to move on to the next demand of the curriculum. But there is also the opportunity to move into rather than on. Yes, we may need to cover the material but there is a chance for understanding of a different order when we can linger and fall into the depths of an idea. When we dive in we have a better chance of finding the whole story or pattern of the discipline rather than merely the facts that lie on the surface.

Beauty is glazed over or drawn out depending on the quality of attention we give it. The contemplative mind and beautiful mind work together. The beautiful does not reveal itself *except* by the investment of our attention and openness.

If beauty can serve as nourishment and even medicine, like any medicine can it also serve as poison? For example, a young girl's introjection (swallowing whole) of the media images of beauty that she can never live up to becomes toxic. Or the flash that we think will satisfy and complete us but does not ever quite do it leaves us hungry and looking for more. Like fast food, "fast beauty" may keep us running but may not nourish us in the way we hope or need in the long run. In this day of hyper access to sound, image, and information bites, "beauty" can engender merely a reaction rather than an experience.

The quick flash of an image designed to grab our attention—sex, violence, and so forth—activates the amygdala, part of the brain responsible for wrestling with emotion. We can have an instinctual response to try to grab more, fall into a kind of titillation without ever moving to a full-bodied, full-minded experience. We know how to turn ourselves on (as do marketers), but that quickly sated desire does not quite satisfy. It may lack the depth of beauty and tends toward addiction rather than sustenance. The problem is intensity without harmony as we become fixated on a narrow bandwidth of intense stimulation instead of a quality of presence. Technology provides abundant access to intensities but not integration, harmony, or balance. These require more presence, more balance, more mind.

Are we awake to what is before us or are we just going through the motions? Whether a glimpse into history, the shape of geometry, the taste of our meal, or the turn of a phrase, the lesson from beauty is that depth, richness, and nourishment in learning requires our engagement, our presence.

BEING BEAUTY

If beauty is so embedded within human consciousness, beyond the art class or the prom dress, where else does it belong in schooling? First and foremost, beauty works through the emotions. It builds a closer link between feeling and thinking. It activates interest, even passion and wonder, and then raises questions. What makes this more beautiful than that? What draws me to this? Are a few sparse lines of Picasso's drawing of a bull "true," capturing some essence that is deeply satisfying, and if so how is this so? How can I have more of this feeling I get in the presence of beauty: awe, love, inspiration, goodness, perfection, and so forth? In this sense beauty joins with considerations of quality, meaning, understanding, imagination, discernment, and self-reflection, capacities needed for the beautiful mind.

Educator Joe Winston argues that the likes of Shakespeare will not be understood by students or teachers and hence not valued until they experience the beauty of the writing. "Learning through beauty is here associated with joy, hope and fulfillment, as motivating a quest for understanding based upon our deepest desires.[20] . . . It is built on a tradition of ideas that explicitly does not confine beauty to the arts, but sees it as evident in human action, human character, in the natural world, in ideas, philosophy, and the foundational principles of science."[21]

When asked to describe an influential teacher, Linda, now a successful teacher herself, understood that it was something about *being beauty*, that lived experience of being touched and immersed, that transformed a lesson into something extraordinary.

> It was an English class, an American mid-century poetry class. The way the guy read the poems, just to demonstrate. He was so completely into them. He was an older guy, looked like it was probably his last year of teaching . . . it was just sort of haunting. I felt *he was living this experience with the poem rather than just teaching it.* And I don't know if that's something I can try to bring in or not but sometimes I feel that in some of the texts I have students

read, I can't have his passion but sometimes I still *feel* the experience at least.
He was feeling it as he was teaching it.

By the way, Linda teaches neither in poetry nor in the humanities in general; she teaches in the human sciences.

Beauty activates desire, and desire reaches for satisfaction and in so doing provides intrinsic motivation. The modern world, claims Richard Sennett in his book *The Craftsman*, has two key methods for urging us to work hard and work well: competition against others, and a moral imperative to do work for the sake of the community.[22] Both approaches are employed in educational practice, and both have their difficulties.

As an alternative or complement, the self-directed and deeply satisfying and fulfilling experience that comes from doing something with quality, with beauty—a well-crafted paragraph, painting, even a mathematical proof— provides self-sustaining motivation. The motivation needed to develop craftsmanship and mastery in writing, speaking, building a chair, designing an experiment, drawing a cat is deepened not merely by wanting to be first in the class, but especially by the intrinsic satisfaction of beauty or quality. To capture just the right arc in the arm of the chair, the flight of the ball, or the turn of a phrase is to find self-reinforcing pleasure at the beauty and satisfaction of doing a good job for its own sake.

Beauty tends to invite replication. That is, when we see something that is beautiful in some way we want to imitate it, capture it, to be it. Appreciation leads to a desire to both replicate and create. Therefore exploring examples of quality and beauty can provide a magnetizing and catalyzing effect.

We try to emulate the moves of our hero on the basketball court or the fashion runway. We fall in love with a song and try to sing it or play it until we get it just right or as right as we can. In fact, we may devote an enormous amount of concentrated energy on trying to get it right. In such absorbed activity the process becomes more *autotelic*, meaning that the purpose is in doing itself. Self-consciousness recedes as we find ourselves immersed in the activity. The state described as *flow* involves being fully absorbed in the activity at hand, whether working on a math problem, building a chair, or running rapids in a kayak. This state of mind and body is characterized by high concentration on a particular activity, merging action and awareness as we lose a sense of our self and along with it our usual sense of time. This immersion is typically deeply satisfying, and the effort, at times, seems almost effortless—it and we are flowing.[23]

In many ways, contemporary schooling treats curriculum and the process of learning as if it were not substantial or sustaining on its own. Of course it is not sustaining when we do not scratch beneath the surface and instead simply ask for recall for an examination and pledge allegiance to a test. When we have only a superficial meal prepared for a test, it is hard for the mind and heart to get engaged or nourished. But ultimately carrots and sticks—extrinsic motivators—may actually spoil the opportunity for direct relevance and resonance.

Like most children, one of my daughters entered first grade with a natural drive and a sponge-like desire to read and be read to. She was excited about choosing books and really seemed to fall into the stories with that full-bodied fascination that children can have. But her relationship to reading changed in one day, in one moment, when she was told that she could win a gold medal and a pizza if she read (or had read to her) five hundred pages over the next few weeks. This motivational gimmick, though well intentioned I presume (and perhaps initially helpful for some students), assumes that the reward for learning cannot be the experience itself; instead, children should expect a material payoff, a bribe.

So that very first night after the announcement, my daughter, who always looked forward to bedtime reading, seemed to be even more eager to get started. She raced to her bedroom bookshelf and started to pull books off the shelf and toss them quickly on her bed. I did not understand what was happening, as she usually was very thoughtful about choosing just the right story. This night she began choosing books not by interest but by a new algorithm: how many pages are readable in the shortest possible time. She was on the pizza hunt. When we read together that night I did not get the same kind of interesting questions and ruminations about the story (e.g., "I would never do what Jane was doing, I would . . ."; "I wonder what it was like for the prince to live on his own planet?"). Instead, I consistently heard: "How many pages is that book?"

This was a stunning change from quality to quantity. The beauty of illustrations, of language, of narrative evaporated under the pressure to reduce this experience to the number of pages read. What was diminished was the chance for depth. It literally took years for her intrinsic motivation toward reading to recover from the programming that leads children to believe they are to get some "thing" for learning. At its best, this cultivates performance-oriented motivation, which is useful but limited, and tends to obscure learning-oriented motivation, which is deepest and most self-sustaining. Performance-oriented motivation is reinforced by a variety of typical practices from the structure of the grading system to daily rewards.

Upon her return home from school on another day, this same daughter reported, "I got to go to the treasure box and picked out this [toy or candy] because I finished all my 'must dos' in my learning centers." "What did you do at the learning centers?" I said earnestly. "I forget," she responded honestly. I saw her losing contact with the object of her learning, the thing she is contacting, and the place in her where it connects.

Behavioral management and manipulation, rewards and punishments, have a place in the teacher's toolbox. When the intrinsic value or interest in the material is not readily apparent to the student it may be appropriate to build a temporary bridge between the object of learning and the individual's interest. Times tables did not seem to get learned during the hustle of the school year and so we thought this a good task over summer vacation. We were traveling and my daughter asked if there was some work she could do during the trip to earn some spending money. The mighty dollar worked as the bridge to get this learning moving, with little prompting, as evidenced by her question from the back seat: "Can we do sixes now?" In the classroom, extrinsic motivational techniques, positive recognition, playful competition, learning games, gold medals, and treasure boxes, can build a temporary if precarious bridge of contact between student and task. But too often they replace the deeper efforts to motivate from the inside out as when we cultivate rich material and interesting applications, and match student concerns and capacities, which make learning relevant, resonant, lifelong, and even beautiful.

A BLISS STATION

Beauty can serve as medicine. Simply beholding beauty can be transformative; a bouquet of flowers brightens a day, time in nature seems to feed us, gorgeous surroundings or a stunning meal brightens our senses and our mood. Beauty provides a bliss station, a restorative touchstone. We turn on some music or behold an image that is special to us and find renewal, comfort, inspiration, and hope. Perhaps there is no more powerful and enduring source of beauty than nature. Nature serves as inspiration and nourishment.

The emergent episteme is more closely tied to nature than the previous mechanistic one. Nowhere is diversity and integration, parts and wholes, individuality and interrelatedness more readily apparent and thus the most available teacher for this expanded way of knowing. There is something about nature that resonates with us deeply and directly: "Nature is on the inside," says Cezanne. "Quality, light, color, depth, which are there before us, are there only because they awaken an echo in our body and because the body welcomes them."[24] In this sense, we are not just on the earth we are of it. Our name, *human*, reminds us of our origin. The word comes from *humus*, which means *earth*.

As if to remind us that our relationship with nature is very special, moments of ecstasy are most frequently reported as being "triggered" by nature.[25] For example, at age eleven, Debbie was by herself on her swing set. As she described to me,

> I was looking up at the sky, just watching. I don't know how it happened, but all of a sudden it all opened up to me. I don't know how to say it, but I felt everything was perfect and connected. I can't say I was thinking anything—

it's like there was no room even to think. It felt like my chest could just burst open and fly into a million pieces. It felt like I could explode and be the sun and the clouds.[26]

Powerful moments like these can shape the course of an entire lifetime and help underscore our connection with the world.

When Thomas was eleven his awareness opened in some inexplicable way and formed a centerpoint for the moral orientation that endured throughout his life. His family was having a new home built at the edge of a small town. Downhill from the house was a small creek and across the creek was a meadow.

It was early afternoon in late May when I first wandered down the incline, crossed the creek, and looked out over the scene.

The field was covered with white lilies rising above the thick grass. A magic moment, this experience gave to my life something that seems to explain my thinking at a more profound level than almost any other experience I can remember. It was not only the lilies. It was the singing of crickets and the woodlands in the distance and the clouds in a clear sky. It was not something conscious that happened just then. I went on about my life as any young person might do. Perhaps it was not simply this moment that made such a deep impression upon me. Perhaps it was a sensitivity that was developed throughout my childhood. As the years passed, this moment returns to me and whenever I think about my basic life attitude and the whole trend of my mind and the causes to which I have given my efforts, I seem to come back to this moment and the impact it has had on my feeling for what is real and worthwhile in life.

This early experience, it seems, has become normative for me throughout the entire range of my thinking. Whatever preserves and enhances this meadow in the natural cycles of its transformation is good: whatever opposes this meadow or negates it is not good. My life orientation is that simple. It is also that pervasive. It applies in economics and political orientation as well as in education and religion.[27]

This was the experience of Thomas Berry, a pioneer integrating spirituality, ecology, and culture. His work emphasizes human interconnection with the earth as recognized through a profound sense of reverence.

Our thinking capacity enables us to imagine that we are separated from the world and permits us to live as if we are. Objectivism and reductionism help maintain this distance. The direct experience of nature helps us to reseat ourselves in the world.

The psychological changes that take place in nature have been referred to as the *wilderness effect*. "There is a shift from culturally reinforced, dualism-producing reality processing to a more non-dualistic mode."[28] Our relationship goes beyond a sense of connection to one of unity. As naturalist John

Muir understood: "The sun shines not on us but in us. The rivers flow not past, but through us."[29]

Richard Louv in his book *Last Child in the Woods: Saving Our Children from Nature Deficit Disorder* suggests that the current generation of children may be on the verge of a kind of nature-deficit disorder as the result of overscheduling, the seduction of electronic stimulation, adult fear of litigation, and the loss of uncontrolled natural spaces to explore and freely play in.[30] They and we may be losing touch with the power of direct encounter with nature and the profound learning that comes with it.

Carolyn Toben, founder of The Center for Education, Imagination, and the Natural World in North Carolina, was having a conversation with Thomas Berry and said to him, "We're finding that children seem to know about global warming and climate change, but they often don't know the sound of a bullfrog or the smell of spring rain." Thomas responded:

> Children need to develop within a whole cosmology of the sun, moon, stars; they need to experience mystical moments of dawn and sunset. They need to awaken to a world to relate to as a communion of subjects not to use a collection of objects. Relationships are the primary context of existence, and children need to see us practice a sympathetic presence to the Earth as a means for being in a mutually enhancing relationship to it. Parents need to say to the child: Let's go out into the sunset, let's wade in a creek, let's go meet the trees. Children need to breathe, to inhale with the whole Earth.[31]

There are plenty of wonderful examples that bring nature to schooling; the bottom line is to help bring ourselves and our charges into a direct personal connection with the natural world. A garden outside the classroom at the middle school near my home provides a place to watch and join with creation and notice how this is like and maybe different from our own growth: "A small group of seven-year-olds suddenly stopping on their trail walk one windy fall day to carefully observe a tiny spider web tossing back and forth, and then watching for minutes in silent amazement at the miraculous movements of the spider to repair it."[32] It is this kind of moment of communion and connection with nature that, as Thomas Berry said, "lays down the enduring value of beauty, wonder and intimacy. A sense of the sacred begins here."[33] And so it is not only for students but also for educators: "Like other artists, educators rediscover spirit through turning to the physical world."[34]

Beauty provides a doorway, gateway, or bridge inviting us from one state to another, enabling us to expand our everyday reality and respond to something that is both greater than ourselves and intimately part of us. By entering that doorway and opening into that communion, we are brought closer to the experience of the union between our inner and outer worlds, between the visible and the invisible.

Maybe beauty will save the world.

Attention to beauty or quality is hardwired into human consciousness, providing powerful motivation and meaning. Yet schooling has had a difficult time finding a place for beauty very far outside of the arts. However, beauty is described as central to the process of discovery and creating in the work not only of artists but also of great scientists and across all disciplines. Perception of beauty is both individualized and also universal in some ways, involving both intensity and harmony, differentiation and integration. Beauty reveals itself to the extent that we open to it. It is tied to our ability to be present to what is before us and thus is related to the contemplative mind. States of flow and intrinsic motivation are catalyzed with attention to beauty, quality, and depth. Nature provides one of the most powerful access points to beauty, serving as a bliss station that can enrich both knowledge and values.

NOTES

1. Fyodor Dostoevsky, *The Idiot*, trans. Richard Pevear and Larissa Volokhonsky (New York: Random House, 2001), 382.

2. Charles Darwin, "The Publication of 'The Origin of the Species,'" in *The Life and Letters of Charles* Darwin, ed. Francis Darwin (London: John Murray, 1887), 296.

3. Alfred North Whitehead, *Adventures of Ideas* (New York: Penguin, 1967), 324.

4. C. S. Lewis, *The Weight of Glory* (London: Society for Promoting Christian Knowledge, 1942), 8; preached originally as a sermon in the Church of St. Mary the Virgin, Oxford, UK, on June 8, 1942.

5. William Lipscomb, "Aesthetic Aspects of Science," in *The Aesthetic Dimension of Science: 1980 Nobel Conference*, ed. D.W. Curtin (New York: Philosophical Library, 1982), 19.

6. Robert Augros and George Stanciu, *The New Story of Science: Mind and the Universe* (Lake Bluff, IL: Regnery Gateway, 1984), 39.

7. Henri Poincaré, *Science and Method* (Mineola, NY: Dover, 2003), 22; original work published 1914.

8. Joe Winston, *Beauty and Education* (New York: Routledge, 2011), 13.

9. Jad Abumrad, "Yellow Fluff and Other Curious Encounters," audio podcast, *Radiolab*. Season 5, episode 5, December 12, 2008, http://www.radiolab.org/2009/jan/12/.

10. Abraham J. Heschel, *God in Search of Man* (New York: Octagon Books, 1972), 36; original work published 1955.

11. Alfred North Whitehead, *Process and Reality*, ed. David Griffin and Donald Sherburne (New York: Simon & Schuster, 1978); and Donald Sherburne, *A Key to Whitehead's Process and Reality* (London: Macmillan, 1966), 216.

12. Alfred North Whitehead, *Adventures of Ideas* (New York: Penguin, 1967), 252.

13. Ibid.

14. Brian Henning, "Re-Centering Process Thought: Recovering Beauty in A. N. Whitehead's Late Work," in *Beyond Metaphysics? Explorations in Alfred North Whitehead's Late Thought* (New York: Rodopi, 2010), 202.

15. Whitehead, *Process and Reality*, 22.

16. Sherburne, *Key to Whitehead's Process and Reality*, 216.

17. Alfred North Whitehead, *Modes of Thought* (New York: Simon & Schuster, 1968). 60.

18. Tobin Hart, *The Four Virtues: Presence, Heart, Wisdom, Creation* (Hillsboro, OR: Beyond Words/Atria, 2014), 7.

19. William Blake, "The Marriage of Heaven and Hell," in *Blake: Complete Writings*, ed. Geoffrey Keynes (Oxford, UK: University Press, 1966), 154.

20. Joe Winston, *Beauty and Education* (New York: Routledge, 2011), 18.

21. Ibid.,18–19.

22. Richard Sennett, *The Craftsman* (New Haven, CT: Yale University Press, 2009).

23. Mihaly Csikszentmihalyi, *Flow: The Psychology of Optimal Experience* (New York: Harper, 2008).

24. Maurice Merleau-Ponty, "Eye and Mind," trans. Carleton Dallery, in *The Primacy of Perception: And Other Essays on Phenomenological Psychology, the Philosophy of Art, History and Politics*, ed. James Edie (Evanston, IL: Northwestern University Press, 1964), 164.

25. Marghanita Laski, *Ecstasy: A Study of Some Secular and Religious Experiences* (London: Cresset Press, 1968).

26. Tobin Hart, *The Secret Spiritual World of Children* (Novato, CA: New World Library, 2003), 11.

27. Thomas Berry, *The Great Work: Our Way Into the Future* (New York: Bell Tower, 1999), 12–13.

28. Robert Greenway, "The Wilderness Effect and Ecopsychology," in *Ecopsychology*, ed. Theodore Roszak, Mary Gomes, and Allen Kanner (San Francisco: Sierra Club, 1995), 131.

29. John Muir, *John of the Mountains: The Unpublished Journals of John Muir*, ed. Linnie Marsh Wolfe (Madison, WI: University of Wisconsin Press, 1979), 92; original work published 1938.

30. Richard Louv, *Last Child in the Woods: Saving Our Children from Nature Deficit Disorder* (Chapel Hill, NC: Algonquin Books, 2005).

31. Carolyn Toben, "A Child Awakens," in *Only the Sacred: Transforming Education in the 21st Century*, ed. Peggy Whalen-Levitt (Greensboro, NC: The Center for Education, Imagination, and the Natural World, 2011), 18.

32. Ibid., 17.

33. Ibid., 19.

34. Mary Caroline Richards, *Toward Wholeness: Rudolf Steiner Education in America* (Middleton, CT: Wesleyan University Press, 1980), 79.

Chapter Four

Embodied Mind

> We are deluged with facts, but we have lost, or are losing, our human ability to feel them. Which means that we have lost or are losing our ability to comprehend the facts of our experience.
>
> —Archibald MacLeish[1]

Despite our sometime obsession with the body, especially some bodies, we have underestimated its role in knowing. There is a long tradition in the West, from Plato to Augustine to Descartes and beyond, of trying to detach ourselves from the body, including the body of nature. Our physical body has been perceived as: a container of suffering—the prison house of the soul for Plato; the throbbing source of moral failure as Augustine understood; and, for Descartes, a machine on which the head rides around. As a result the body, its feelings, sensations, and nonlinguistic perceptions, has been understood as primarily extracurricular in contemporary education. The directness of a felt sense or gut intuition, the clasp of hand to tool, and the scent of the day have been mostly irrelevant to objective, abstract concepts and categories.

As part of the dismissal of the body, the modernist emphasis on objectivity—seeing what is on the outside—has pushed subjective perception—sensing what is on the inside—far to the background. (Although the subjectivity of the romantics found some shelter in the humanities.)

The result is that we build curriculum and pedagogy emphasizing abstract ideas and objectivity; but here is the rub. Development involves not only differentiation toward abstraction but also integration, not only objectivity but also subjectivity, not only cognitive transcendence but also inclusion of previously developed capabilities. We do not lose our capacity or need to feel, sense, and commune with the world around us in favor of a detached, abstract categorical understanding, but for the most part modernist education has encouraged us to do just this.

As a general trend, time for recess, the arts, subjectivity, craftsmanship, hands-on, in-the-world learning has shrunk in order to provide more emphasis on the important tasks of learning abstract curriculum. It is no wonder that attention and motivation become problems when our bodies are taken out of the loop of learning. If we do lose that ground of lived experience the world becomes, in Whitehead's words, "a dull affair, soundless, scentless, colorless."[2] The result is an abbreviated approach to mind.

In addition to the physical body itself, to be embodied means that we exist in the world. In the premodern worldview we were embedded in the world, part of the *anima mundi*—the world soul. We were immersed in and at the whim of the forces—divine, terrestrial, archetypal—of a living world.

The enlightenment freed us from this enmeshment. The modern mind separates the self from the world, gradually differentiating us from it. However, in so doing the modern world has become disenchanted, to use Max Weber's term.[3] No longer a world alive with meaning, magic, metaphor, the world becomes largely a collection of objects, inert and available for our manipulation and only our meaning making, devoid of any meaning of its own.

Beyond the raft of possibilities and problems that this worldview has wrought on the world, it is especially our consciousness that pays. Cultural historian Richard Tarnas says it this way: "The achievement of human autonomy has been paid for by the experience of human alienation."[4] This great ability to objectify has left us in our heads, outside or above the world and our bodies, searching for a way back in. Today we are not looking for a description of life; we are increasingly hungry for an experience of being alive. That experience comes from being embodied in the world.

The path ahead for consciousness and culture is to find a way back into the world and into our bodies. The solution is not a return to the premodern worldview any more than it is to return to the preverbal state of childhood. Instead the challenge is to reunite body and mind, world and self in a new level of integration. When we do, the body returns as a legitimate source of knowing in a living universe.

MIND-BODY REUNITED

The modernist conception emphasizing abstraction and objectification has been a mind separate from the body, but recent evidence points to a different reality.

Mind-body medicine is coming to recognize that the mind and body are intertwined. How we think can affect our body. Frustration and pessimism, for example, impact immune response that makes us vulnerable to everything from a cold to cancer. Likewise, the well-understood placebo effect demonstrates that, for example, in a large percentage of participants, believing that they have taken a new drug, even when they have not, causes the changes that the actual drug was supposed to induce.

But the process also works in the opposite direction: the body impacts our thinking. If, for example, we have a cold or a pain, we may notice that our concentration wanes; but it goes deeper than this.

In the 1980s neuroscientist Candace Pert uncovered something in the last place a good brain scientist would expect to find it. Her research revealed neuropeptides and their receptor sites, presumed to exist only in the brain and central to our thinking processes, in the gut. It begged the question of whether the gut and perhaps other parts of the body were capable of thinking too. As Pert concluded, "I can no longer make a strong distinction between the brain and the body."[5]

Today we recognize that there is a highly complex, bidirectional gut-brain system, referred to as the enteric nervous system, impacting affect, motivation, and higher cognitive functions including decision making.[6] Some psychiatrists, for example, are now prescribing probiotics to increase bacteria in the gut in order to treat "mind problems" like obsessive compulsive disorder and anxiety, recognizing that the gut is somehow integrated with mind.[7] Of course this extends in familiar ways as we are recognizing the influence of things like diet and stress on cognition and mood.[8]

Although we do not have it all mapped out, or even close, we are beginning to put our parts back together. That is, mind and body exist not separate from one another as Descartes implied, not even as connected as early mind-body medicine understood, but as a complex, interactive unity.[9]

One function the body provides is a kind of immediate cognition or intuition. Our bodies know things before our mind registers them. In one study, University of Iowa scientists asked participants to play a card game involving four decks of cards, two blue and the other two red. Each card either wins you money or costs you money. The goal is to turn over cards one at a time from any deck to maximize your winnings. The red cards offer some high rewards and high costs. In fact, what you don't know to start with is that the game is rigged so you can only win by turning over cards from the blue deck. As you play the game, how long will it take to figure this out?

As it turns out, participants in this Iowa study get a hunch, an idea, after they have turned over about fifty cards. Although they cannot say why, they know they prefer the blue deck. In time reasoning kicks in and we may start to develop a theory or explanation about it.

However, there was one more aspect of the experiment. The researchers hooked up each participant to measure their galvanic skin response (GSR) (electrical conductivity of the skin—sweat) in the palm of their hands. The more stress we experience, the more sweat we register, the higher the GSR. What they found is that the participants started to generate a stress response to the red cards by the tenth card. Their actions also correspondingly started to favor the blue decks at about that same time. But they did not have an idea or a hunch that any of this was happening until the fiftieth card, and it took eighty cards before they formed a clear theory about it. [10] Their bodies knew before their thinking made sense of it.

While we often assume thought generates feelings, it looks like thought, emotion, and sensation work in a more integrative and bidirectional fashion. A thought might indeed lead to a feeling and felt sense but at the same time a physical reaction may be just as likely to lead to a thought. For example, in the Iowa study it looks like the chain of experience goes like this: physiological reaction (increase in sweat), felt sense (a vague hunch or gut sense), a feeling ("I feel more comfortable with blue cards"), an idea or concept ("It's the blue cards!").

Staying "in" or attuned to our bodies gives us a profound source of information about the world. Listening to those gut feelings, incorporating our hunches, feeling our way into the question, and thinking it through combine to enrich our knowing. Our thinking is actually a more sensory, body-infused process than the dualist conception assumes.

Our sensory-emotional system appears to have evolved as a way of responding to the outside world, such as when we have an immediate reaction to a threat. Our body often "knows" and responds to something before we are aware of it. Feelings—"I'm scared." "I feel guilty." "I love this!"—are basically the conscious sense of that body-based knowing, whereas emotional reactions are thought to be largely body-based reactions out of conscious awareness. This sophisticated emotional system has been mistakenly pushed to the sideline, seen as merely secondary, largely separate from and simply controlled by the more elevated thought process, what neuroscientist Antonio Damasio referred to as Descartes' error—I think, therefore I am. [11] The result has been a loss of attention to the sensitivity and integration of the emotional-sensory-bodily world and instead a tendency to "live in our heads."

As William James understood more than one hundred years ago, thought is an embodied experience. That is, there is a continuous thinking-feeling process or flow that is in transaction with the environment and tied to the body's monitoring of its own states. Whether we are writing a paper or talking with a lover or painting a picture, we feel how our thinking is going. We feel when it is blocked. We feel when it moves forward and how it moves. [12]

Psychologist Eugene Gendlin wondered what made psychotherapy work. He knew that sometimes it did, fulfilling its promise for help and healing, but just as often despite the time, expense, and commitment, it seemed to do very little. In time he discovered that there was something particular happening in transformative therapy. In clients for whom therapy made a difference there was sometimes insight into their difficulties, new commitments to change behavior, and the like, but the thing that made a difference was their body. That is, change was catalyzed by an awareness of what Gendlin called a "felt sense." While one may have an intellectual insight, it was this felt bodily sense that engendered change. He understands the body and the person as a unified system and that the body has a subtler take on what is going on. He developed a method called focusing, which directs our awareness to the body, beneath the surface of feelings and thoughts, in order to pay attention to those inner sensations and gain insight. [13]

If, as mind-body medicine and body-oriented psychotherapy suggests, consciousness is indeed embodied in this way, then education is served by including the body, especially this felt sense, in our lesson plans. (By the way, most of the signals from the body—that gut feeling and so forth—enter the brain through the right hemisphere.)

This inner listening provides a simple and flexible method for directing our attention inward in order to tune into those vague sensations in our body. Whether in trying to sort out an answer to a homework problem or picking a research paper topic or navigating our social relations we can invite students to listen to their bodies:

> *Consider a concern or question that you have. Be quiet for a few moments and shift inward, into your body, perhaps in your torso or elsewhere that seems right to you or that you seem drawn to. Where in your body do you notice that issue? What is the felt sense under the feelings and beneath any thoughts? Stay with it and notice what arises as you give it your gentle attention. What are the qualities of that sensation? How is it changing as you notice it? In time you might try to name it or its qualities. As you stay with the felt sense what arises?*

The felt sense of the body complements the typical linguistic thought process, bringing enriched knowing to any enterprise at any moment.

In addition to shifting our attention to that felt sense, moving the body may also help open the mind.

Lara was a willing student but could not seem to make sense of her math classes, struggling mightily but without anything that could be considered success. She just could not seem to get it. One day she was moving, spinning, and dancing, and something suddenly clicked. She realized that she spontaneously wanted to move in certain ways in response to a math question and then began experimenting further. Remarkable to her, when she did move she seemed to actually understand the math. There was something about the movement that apparently activated her mind in fresh ways. She went on to complete a college degree in mathematics alongside training in Russian classical ballet. She works professionally now using integrative movement to help children with special needs and chronic pain patients and to help optimize well-being and performance for anyone. [14]

Educational kinesthesiology offers a series of physical exercises and an understanding that moving the body helps keep attention alive, may decrease immediate stress response, and helps shift consciousness such as when we feel intellectually stuck or overwhelmed. Certain practices, such as any bilateral activity (walking is such an activity), may help synchronize or balance activity in left and right brain hemispheres. At the very least these simple activities can be a playful way to return the body to learning as we shift mood and attention. [15]

Our body-mind operates as a system, so activity in one aspect of our physical and mental being may very well activate something in another. The entire fields of body-oriented psychotherapy, yoga and body-work, movement-based therapies, the effect of exercise on biochemistry and stress, and so much else often cast as alternative or complementary medicine are largely based on an understanding that the body holds and effects consciousness. So moving the body to move learning is not far-fetched.

COMING TO OUR SENSES

In addition to the value of inner felt sense and of movement, we know the world most directly through our senses. Leonardo da Vinci claimed that "all our knowledge has its origin in our senses." [16] But the modernist emphasis on abstraction has made the senses second-class in favor of a world once removed through language and categorical understanding. Without the grounding of the senses the world becomes virtual instead of visceral as we drift further from the ground of being. One opportunity the embodied mind presents is to reappraise the value of the senses.

Blinded and deafened by illness at fifteen months, Helen Keller struggled for six years in a dark world where neither her own existence nor the world around her made any sense; she grew more alienated and detached. Her salvation came not only in the form of her teacher Annie Sullivan but from a deep connection between the sensual world and the world of language. Her opening took place at the age of seven:

> We walked down the path to the well-house, attracted by the fragrance of the honeysuckle with which it was covered. Someone was drawing water and my teacher placed my hand under the spout. As the cool stream gushed over one hand she spelled into the other the word water, first slowly, then rapidly. I stood still, my whole attention fixed upon the motions of her fingers. Suddenly I felt a misty consciousness as of something forgotten—a thrill of returning thought; and somehow the mystery of language was revealed to me. I knew then that "w-a-t-e-r" meant the wonderful cool something that was flowing

over my hand. That living word awakened my soul, gave it light, hope, joy, set it free. [17]

This moment describes a profound cognitive leap, essentially a bridge built to the world through the integration of sensation and syllable.

We recognize the value of senses at the high end: a wine connoisseur, a symphonic conductor, a mechanic whose ear is tuned to the subtle sounds of an engine, all represent ways in which awareness in the form of sensory perception can bring more depth to knowing. Individuals who live close to the land may develop keen observational skills, and great naturalists like Charles Darwin and John Muir notice subtleties that others may miss. Such fine-honed sensitivity helps us recognize the potential of the senses. Opportunities in schooling for careful sensory observation raise the profile of senses.

Howard described himself as struggling and lost as a learner until one day in his biology classroom:

> Mr. Scroggins was a southern man in a California public school. He would get us to draw what we saw. As we looked at slides under the microscope he had us fold unlined paper in half and draw three pictures maximum on each page. I could use colored pencils. This drawing got me to focus on *seeing* more than analyzing abstractions or simply memorizing words. I remember thinking that if I ever saw mitosis floating by in my day-to-day life I would recognize it because it was now embedded in my mind. I remember the phases and I could see it because I could draw it. This all caught me by surprise.

His confidence and his capacity made a huge leap thanks to bringing the senses and the abstractions together.

In order to activate more of the body-mind, we might ask students in any discipline to draw a response to a particular problem rather than use language exclusively. In a small section of a university psychology class, my students are asked to use Play-Doh to depict (and then later explain) an aspect of personality when we are working on that section in our text. I am always amazed after some playfulness by the silence and intensity of concentration that comes over the room as they fall into this kindergarten-like assignment. There is something about the tactile nature of it that takes them deep inside to access material in a surprising way. Their depictions, molded and then spoken or written, are rich with understanding. The exercise provides an opportunity to integrate idea and form, language and feel. Afterward many ask earnestly if they can keep the Play-Doh.

In literature, great description engages the body via the senses—"It was a dark and stormy night"—to evoke a visceral experience of the event. Social scientists engage in thick phenomenological description to capture the body of experience of the scene they are viewing or the person they are interviewing. Great poetry or other art often mixes and joins senses in a synesthetic event.

Early in life we become conditioned as to how to talk about (and thus experience) our senses as fairly segregated from one another. We describe a meal by its taste, music by its sound. But senses are not so distinct. During moments of expanded awareness nearly everyone can have synesthetic experiences—merged or multi-senses—and young children seem to have them often. We discover that some of our great artists and poets appear to maintain synesthesia. This was the source of their great metaphors or unique ways of both taking in and representing the world. "I heard flowers that sounded, and saw notes that shone," reports eighteenth-century philosopher Saint-Martin.[18] Synesthetic impressions occur not only in perceiving outwardly—a blue sky or the sound of a bird—but also inwardly, as with the birth of an idea. Mozart described his process of composing in this way: "I can see the whole of it [musical composition] at a single glance in my mind, as if it were a beautiful painting . . . in which way I do not hear it in my imagination at all as a succession . . . but all at once."[19]

Cognitive neuroscience is coming to understand just how valuable multisensory perception is.

> The key to robust perception is the combination and integration of multiple sources of sensory information. This is because no information-processing system, neither technical nor biological, is powerful enough to "perceive and act" accurately under all conditions.[20]

Synesthesia may represent a reminder of our capacities—the multisensory human. The French philosopher Maurice Merleau-Ponty tells us that we are naturally synesthetic, but culture has shifted "the center of gravity of experience, so that we have unlearned how to see, hear, and generally speaking feel, in order to deduce [what we sense]."[21] That is, education and culture not only teach what we are supposed to know but especially how we know, the style of knowing that is considered acceptable and associated with status and the search for truth. This can overly mediate our experience with our mental categories.

The implication then for the front edge of human development is to become more fully multisensory beings, reawakening the delicate sensitivity of all our ways of knowing and in so doing return the body to a legitimate source of knowing. When we do, perception becomes more robust and reliable and our metaphors more meaty.

We can dismantle the fences of our own perception by paying close attention to our senses, like Howard's drawing a cell. We can also expand our sensory habits by asking questions such as: "Does that sound have a shape?" "Draw what that song feels like in your body and then describe it to us." "What is the shape of this taste?" "What does that idea look like?" Playful, even ridiculous at first blush, this divergent breaking up of categorical perception opens up both the body and new possibilities. In so doing we may regain more richness and unexpected connections that the senses have to offer.

JUST DO IT

Our powers of observation, of refined discrimination, self-discipline, deduction and calculation, systematic experimentation, and problem solving all are activated when we embody an idea in an action in some way.

Information must be utilized, applied, integrated in one's mind and life in order for it to move toward mastery. We actually have to "do math" in order to learn it: memorizing formulae is insufficient; we must practice reading in order to master it; and so on. And often, mastery comes only when knowledge is applied in the world.

Sebastian, a graduate student at a premier engineering and science research university, never understood basic fractions until he began to experiment with woodworking in college. Only when he needed to use the math to solve problems, to measure, cut, and calculate in order to build his ideas, did it click for him. Mary remembers the pleasure and sense of accomplishment in learning fractions as a child by making reduced-sized recipes, a single cream puff or cupcake after school. Both of these students turned information into knowledge by applying it in their world.

Krishnamurti says, "Learning is doing, so in the very act of doing you are learning."[22] Progressive educators have a long tradition of attempting to provide a more immediate relationship to the object of learning. Rousseau advocated learning "naturally" and by doing.[23] His call was taken up by Pestalozzi, who focused on learning through direct concrete experience.[24] Dewey emphasized learning by experience and through cooperative endeavors.[25] Some of this insight has certainly been incorporated into the mainstream. For example, in science education, we see initiatives to bring teachers and students into the "field" of their subject by experimenting and solving problems firsthand. They may work on a problem of erosion in a nearby river by visiting the site, taking measurements, constructing models, and so forth. And many enrichment programs emphasize problem-based design. This gives immediacy to abstract information and necessitates its use in practice.

Projects can help bring learning to life: "Build a chair out of cardboard." "Make a positive difference in someone's life." "Design a more energy efficient building." "What is autism like?" "How could our classroom be more successful?" "Design a website that . . ." In a classroom (or a workplace) framing the learning environment as an opportunity for discovery and creative problem solving, rather than simply downloading data, embodies learning. Most disciplines lend themselves to this. One shoe never fits all, and while research on project-based design is generally very positive, it does require skilled and flexible teachers. [26]

This voice of direct contact too often gets overwhelmed by curricular demands, scheduling limitations, and primarily by the assumption that we can download material into an empty vessel or memory bank and adequately evaluate knowledge through a multiple-choice exam. The accountancy movement and its accompanying anxiety push project-based, hands-on learning into the closet. Not only do ideas remain inert without firsthand contact, but students can easily remain inert themselves, listless or mechanical, partially asleep.

In the 1970s the Finnish government decided that in order to be relevant in the new global marketplace, one in which manufacturing was no longer the mainstay for a country without vast natural resources and inexpensive labor, theirs needed to be a knowledge-based economy. To get it up to speed they understood the need to renovate the educational system. The results thirty plus years down the road: student test scores in all three areas of testing—math, reading, and science—are among the highest in the world. Finland is also at or near the top on quality of life, which is clearly not the case among other top scoring nations like Singapore and South Korea, which rely on long hours, lots of memorization, plenty of competition, and testing. But how does Finland do it?

Finnish children play more: seventy-five minutes a day in elementary school recess as opposed to the average of twenty-seven minutes in the United States. Finnish schools mandate lots of arts and crafts. According to scholar Samuel Abrams, "Students in grades one through nine spend from four to eleven periods each week taking classes in art, music, cooking, carpentry, metalwork, and textiles. These classes provide natural venues for learning math and science, nurture critical cooperative skills, and implicitly cultivate respect for people who make their living working with their hands." [27]

There is no standardized curriculum. Teachers design their own classes using a national curriculum only as a guide and resource. No standardized curriculum is bad enough, but perhaps most unsettling to prevailing American assumptions about school reform is that Finland has no standardized exams. The only exception is if students intend to go on to university they take the National Matriculation Exam at the end of what is roughly equivalent to high school in the United States. Instead of centralized testing regimes, teachers assess students in their classrooms using tests that they create themselves. Students are graded on an individualized basis. Students are not held back, because of the overwhelming social stigma that would result, but instead are given additional help.

Along with testing and accountability, competition is one of the corner-stones of an American approach to educational improvement. Not so in Fin-land. The goal for Finnish school reform was not super achievement; instead it was equity, seeing that all children are well educated regardless of region or class. The result, however, is this exceptional performance.

But unlike the United States, Finland has a fairly homogenous population. (Although many U.S. states would be comparable both in terms of size and racial homogeneity.) It begs the question of whether a style of educational reform dependent on cooperation and equity rather than competition and performance is applicable in a place like the United States. Samuel Abrams has addressed the effects of size and homogeneity on a nation's education performance by comparing Finland with another Nordic country: Norway. Like Finland, Norway is small and not especially diverse overall, but unlike Finland it has taken an approach to education that is more American than Finnish. The result in Norway: mediocre national performance.[28]

THE POWER OF PLACE

In 2007 the residents of tiny Walton, Kansas, wanted to save their local elementary school and perhaps their town along with it. With only sixty students left, the school was no longer cost-effective and was slated to shut its doors. But the Newton district, of which the school was a part, took a risk. Instead of shuttering the school they radically reconstituted it as The Walton 21st Century Rural Life Center, a charter school with a very different curric-ulum.

The school, and much of Kansas, is oriented around farming. This does not mean teaching children to be farmers but instead using the life around them to learn. And, so it seems, "there is almost nothing in elementary education that can't be explained by relating it to cows and plows." For example,

> The students sell eggs produced by a small coop of hens. Every morning they rush out to collect and wash the eggs, inspect them for cracks, and box them for sale for $2 a dozen. (They recently bought a sheep with the proceeds.) The students learn how to tell the difference between a Delaware Blue and a Rhode Island Red, but also about profit and loss, and when the chickens don't lay enough to meet projections, supply and demand.
>
> Walton kids take rulers and protractors to everything from tractor tires to goat horns. They learn their ounces, cups and pints by measuring grain for animal feed and oats for granola. . . . The fourth graders recently made a mockup of a wind turbine, learning about things like torque and the behavior of different blades. . . . [I]n the school's prairie garden, native Kansas plants prompt lessons about soil composition, weather patterns, and ecology.[29]

Today the school is flourishing, and student test scores jumped to the top 5 percent of all schools in the state.

Part of what makes Walton succeed is not only the project-based design but also that it is "place-based," embodied or integrated within the local community. Place-based learning is about using the natural and social community that we are embedded in as the basis for education. As with the Walton school, any environment, both natural and cultural, that is at our back door can be fertile ground for making learning relevant, intimate, and alive. Whether considering local stream erosion or changing population demographics or oral history, this approach embodies learning in the middle of our home base.[30]

Far from Kansas, Brazilian educator Paulo Freire recognized the social and economic oppression of peasants in his native Brazil.[31] His approach toward social justice was a kind of place-based literacy. Emphasizing critical reflection of the local economic and power dynamics, his approach explicitly taught language and implicitly taught empowerment and social justice. Any local concern (and even nonlocal, given our current global access to one another and to information) may serve as a kind of place-based trailhead for learning.

CRAFTSMANSHIP

For three and a half billion years or so life on earth has been adapting. In his book *Learning from the Octopus*, ecologist and security expert Rafe Sagarin suggests that in these times of incredible demands ranging from terrorism to environmental catastrophe to pandemic disease we can learn something about solving problems from the way nature does it.[32] This has implications not only for post–9/11 security but also for how we educate, especially in a world that is so incredibly dynamic, unpredictable, and interrelated. What does the octopus or the tide pool or nature at large have to teach us about education?

When considering the natural world, one of the first and most obvious things noticed is the diversity of responses (including species) that have evolved to meet various needs or demands from the environment. Diversity and divergence are the motor behind evolution, and so the most direct lesson from nature may be that rather than work toward single responses, single right answers, and right procedures that so predominate educational curriculum, it is diversity that generates new possibilities to be experimented with in nature and the classroom. Of course sometimes the answer or the procedure is the whole point, but not with everything and not always. The value of diversity and divergence is considered in some detail in the chapter on the imaginative mind.

Second, all natural systems have a feedback loop built in. If their adaptation works they thrive, if it does not they may be in peril. Being sure to construct an educational arrangement whereby feedback is built in and fairly immediate so that we can recalibrate, adjust, and continue to learn helps get learning moving. This is an environment where the need for one right perfect answer is modulated with the need for process and experimentation. If one thing does not work well, find out as fast as you can and try something else. Feedback is best when it is quick, concrete, and clear.

In addition to diverse responses and natural feedback loops, Sagarin demonstrates that in the natural world nearly all organisms have symbiotic relationships with others, helping to solve one another's problems. Bees spread pollen in exchange for nectar; lichens are a partnership of fungi, algae, and bacteria, and on and on. The implication for humans, whether at the level of security concerns or for the classroom, is the value of an environment in which cooperation and collaboration can emerge alongside independent effort and friendly competition.

The pursuit of craftsmanship is one way to think about learning that highlights organized creative redundancy and experimentation, feedback, and cooperation.

Like the medieval workshops, classrooms (virtual or otherwise) contain masters (teachers who set the direction and vision for the work), emerging journeymen (those whose talent or growing skill place them at the head of the discipline and therefore are natural aids), and apprentices (those students who are working to learn the new skills).

Whether in learning the use of language or algebra, in taking an engine or an idea apart, developing skills becomes more than information download but can become craft when an appreciation of beauty and quality, process and form join head and hand. The workshop goes beyond passive transmission and instead engenders first-hand engagement, bringing a living exchange between knower and knowledge. Incorporating a writer's workshop model, a problem-focused design, a project-focused orientation, a project in the field, and a hands-on laboratory are among the means to retool the classroom as workshop and learning as craftsmanship.

My friend Kent learned to write in Mr. Monroe's eight-grade English class. Mr. Monroe decided that it would be his mission to make sure his students could write before they entered high school and so he set his class up as a kind of writing boot camp. Essentially it was an on-going writing workshop in which students read one another's papers and offered constructive feedback all the while under the supervision of Mr. Monroe. "This changed my relationship to education," Kent says. "I remember loving to write for his class."

Up to that point in my life every class was set-up in the traditional way—students lined up in rows, and the teacher facing students. Mr. Monroe's classroom was filled with big round tables. He would have us write on a specific topic, and then we'd bring it in and divide up into pairs to review each other's work. I spent a whole year working on my writing and getting the feedback from my peers and from Mr. Monroe. Additionally, I spent that year reading the writings of my co-students, and I learned how to see them with a critical eye and to express this in supportive language. It was also the first time that I remember developing close connections with my classmates, as we were so involved in helping each other learn and grow. I have some fond memories of sitting around those big tables, huddled up with a classmate, discussing the papers that we wrote. In retrospect, it was more like a workshop or lab than a classroom. It was in this setting that I developed a beautiful relationship with writing.

I really learned how to appreciate receiving feedback. Before him, the teacher's pen usually left a message on my papers of "good" or "bad." In Mr. Monroe's class it was all about constructive criticism. I learned to gracefully give and receive feedback. This not only helped in the development of my writing skills, it had a permanent impact on my capacity to learn and grow. Rather than seeing feedback in a negative light, which would have created defensiveness in the process, I learned the beauty and support of quality feedback. I learned to really appreciate hearing the view of others, and to see criticisms as gifts.

In the classroom, too often the obsession with one right answer across so many domains focuses too much on final product and final grade instead of process and thus misses the chance for classrooms to function more as workshops or artist's studios or laboratories where trial and error, experimentation, feedback, and adventure provide the means to develop ideas and skill. Alongside more teaching-for-the-tests, the result of this form of abbreviation is that "neither teachers nor students are willing to undertake risks for understanding; instead they content themselves with correct answer compromises. Under such compromises education is considered a success if students are able to provide answers that are sanctioned as correct."[33] Overemphasis on information acquisition has inadvertently worked against higher-order intellectual skills and led to a constriction of human consciousness.

Craftspeople create something that enters the world in some way that others can touch, use, taste, and see. We can see what works or what flops: feedback. Thanks to today's technology, extended opportunities for more real-world feedback are available; we can take our craft into the wider world. For example, through class-only or real-world blogs students can put their work into the world and with a little luck receive meaningful response.

Author Clive Thompson describes an extremely low-performing school in New Zealand where teachers tried a fresh tack. Recognizing that motivation can change when one is writing on a topic important to them and writing for an audience, students were required to post their own writing on a live Internet blog.

Things started to change when students began to receive comments from other authors. There was a real audience out there, in some cases way out there, as students marveled at receiving a post from Germany or the United States. Thompson reports that when one student reviewed a book online, the author popped up to comment on the review. Students had a real-world audience and the result was a dramatic increase in their motivation. With it, their teachers saw them paying more attention to punctuation, to clarifying their points, and editing in general. They also now were doing the key thing that helps one write better: they were writing more. Their motivation exploded. They were figuring out what to write, how to best convey it to their audience, making sure it was as clear as they could make it, and, perhaps most significantly, they were writing on their own.[34]

Beyond the effect on writing itself, it turns out that writing is also powerfully helpful for improving reading. That is, crafting something in writing helps us understand what we are reading. Literary scholar Steve Graham concludes from analyzing dozens of studies that writing about a text helps us to understand and internalize the material better than "just reading it, reading and rereading it, reading and studying it, reading and discussing it, and receiving reading instruction."[35]

(And by the way, the reading and writing scores for the New Zealand school children improved dramatically.)

We are coming to understand the body and mind as a unified system. No longer merely a source of suffering or a machine, the body is central to knowing. To be embodied means to enter into our life with all the taste and texture, tone and temperature that being human entails. Attunement to felt sense, fresh appreciation for the senses, and the value of activating the mind through movement and activity returns the body to its natural place in learning. Hands-on activity and projects engender an environment that operates more as a craft or artist studio inviting feedback, cooperation, and diversity of response. We exist within a larger community. As such, embodiment means using the immediacy of what is at our back door and at our fingertips.

NOTES

1. Archibald MacLeish, "Poetry and Journalism," in *A Continuing Journey* (Boston: Houghton Mifflin, 1958), 43.

2. Alfred N. Whitehead, *Science and the Modern World* (New York: Macmillan, 1925), 54.

3. Max Weber, "Science as a Vocation," in *Max Weber: Essays on Sociology,* ed. Hans H. Gerth and C. Wright Mills (New York: Oxford University Press, 1946), 139.

4. Richard Tarnas, *Cosmos and Psyche: Intimations of a New World View* (New York: Penguin, 2007), 25.

5. Candace B. Pert, "The Wisdom of the Receptors: Neuropeptides, the Emotions, and Bodymind," *Advance* 3, no. 3 (1986): 16.

6. Emeran A. Mayer, "Gut Feelings: The Emerging Biology of Gut-Brain Communication," *Nature Reviews Neuroscience*, July 13, 2011, doi:10.1038/nrn3071.

7. Carrie Arnold, "Gut Feelings: The Future of Psychiatry May Be Inside Your Stomach," *The Verge*, August 21, 2013, http://mobile.theverge.com/2013/8/21/4595712/gut-feelings-the-future-of-psychiatry-may-be-inside-your-stomach.

8. See, for example, David Perlmutter, *Grain Brain: The Surprising Truth About Wheat, Carbs, and Sugar—Your Brain's Silent Killers* (New York: Little, Brown, 2013).

9. Henry Dreher, *Mind-Body Unity: A New Vision for Mind-Body Science and Medicine* (Baltimore: The Johns Hopkins University Press, 2003).

10. Antoine Bechara, Hanna Damasio, Daniel Tranel, and Antonio R. Damasio, "Deciding Advantageously Before Knowing the Advantageous Strategy," *Science* 275 (1997): 1293–1295; Malcolm Gladwell, *Blink: The Power of Thinking Without Thinking* (New York: Little Brown, 2005).

11. Antonio Damasio, *Descartes' Error: Emotion, Reason, and the Human Brain* (New York: HarperCollins, 1994).

12. Mark Johnson, *The Body in the Mind: The Bodily Basis of Meaning, Imagination, and Reason* (Chicago: University Press, 1990), 102.

13. Eugene Gendlin, *Focusing* (New York: Bantam, 1982).

14. Lara Gillease, "Lara's Integrative Movement," http://www.integrativemovement.com.

15. See, for example, Carla Hannaford, *Smart Moves: Why Learning Is Not All in Your Head* (Salt Lake City, UT: Great River Books, 2007); and Paul E. Dennison and Gail E. Dennison, *Brain Gym: Teacher's Edition* (Ventura, CA: Edu-Kinesthetics, 2010). For annotated research summaries: www.braingym.org/brochures/BG-Research.pdf.

16. Leonardo da Vinci, *Il Codex Trivulzianus,* trans. Anna Maria Brizio (Florence: Giunti Editore, 1980), folio 20v; Fritjof Capra, *The Science of Leonardo* (New York: Doubleday, 2007).

17. Helen Keller, *The Story of My Life* (New York: Doubleday, Page & Co., 1903), 23.

18. As cited in Evelyn Underhill, *Mysticism* (New York: E. P. Dutton, 1961), 7; original work published 1911.

19. As cited in William James, *Principles of Psychology* (New York: Henry Holt, 1893), 255.

20. M. O. Ernst and H. H. Bülthoff, "Merging the Senses into a Robust Percept," *Trends in Cognitive Sciences* 8, no. 4 (2004): 169.

21. Maurice Merleau-Ponty, *Phenomenology of Perception* (New York: Humanities Press, 1962), 205.

22. Jiddu Krishnamurti, *Krishnamurti on Education* (New York: Harper & Row, 1974), 82.

23. Jean-Jacques Rousseau, *Emile*, trans. B. Fosley (New York: E. P. Dutton, 1957); original work published 1762.

24. Heinrich Pestalozzi, *The Education of Man: Aphorisms* (New York: Greenwood, 1951).

25. John Dewey, *Experience and Education* (New York: Macmillan, 1963); original work published 1938.

26. Ted Bredderman, *Effect of Activity-Based Elementary Science on Student Outcomes: A Quantitative Synthesis* (Albany, NY: SUNY Press, 1983); John W. Thomas, *A Review of Research on Project-Based Learning* (San Rafael, CA: The Autodesk Foundation, 2000).

27. Samuel Abrams, "The Children Must Play: What the United States Could Learn from Finland About Education Reform," *The New Republic*, January 28, 2011, http://www.newrepublic.com/article/politics/82329/education-reform-Finland-US.

28. Ibid.

29. Susan Headden, "A Town Turned Classroom: How a Focus on Farming Saved a Rural Kansas School," *Education Sector at American Institutes for Research*, October 11, 2012, www.educationsector.org/publications/town-turned-classroom-how-focus-farming-saved-rural-kansas-school.

30. "Place-Based Learning Offers Opportunities for High-Poverty Rural Schools," *Rural Policy Matters* 13, no. 9 (Washington, DC: The Rural School and Community Trust, 2011).

31. Paulo Freire, *Pedagogy of the Oppressed*, trans. Myra Bergman Ramos (New York: Continuum, 1970). See also, for example, www.promiseofplace.org.

32. Rafe Sagarin, *Learning from the Octopus: How Secrets from Nature Can Help Us Fight Terrorist Attacks, Natural Disasters, and Disease* (New York: Basic Books, 2012).

33. Howard Gardner, *The Unschooled Mind: How Children Think and How Schools Should Teach* (New York: Basic Books, 1991), 150.

34. Clive Thompson, *Smarter Than You Think: How Technology Is Changing Our Minds for the Better* (New York: Penguin, 2013), 184–187.

35. Steven Graham and Michael Herbert, *Writing to Read: Evidence for How Writing Can Improve Reading* (Washington, DC: Alliance for Excellent Education, 2010), 14, carnegie.org/fileadmin/Media/Publications/WritingToRead_01.pdf; Clive Thompson, *Smarter Than You Think*, 184, 314.

Chapter Five

Imaginative Mind

To me—and not many others think so—the real crises in the life of our society is the crisis of the life of the imagination. Far more than we need an intercontinental missile or a moral rearmament of a religious revival, we need to come alive again, to recover the virility of the imagination on which all earlier civilizations have been based.

—Archibald MacLeish[1]

On her fifth day of kindergarten, the day after her fifth birthday, one of my daughters was given a short homework assignment in the form of a pre-printed page that required her to circle the two out of three objects that "belonged together." Each question had a group of three shapes. One group included a small green rectangle, a green triangle, and a red square. "Which two belong together?" She circled the red square and the green rectangle. When I asked her about her choice, she acknowledged that two had the same color, but also understood that two of them had four sides each. The next day at school the assignment was returned to her and her answer to this question was marked incorrect.

Obsession with the right answer misses the opportunity to see questions from multiple vantage points, in this case to understand that different shapes can perform certain functions. My five-year-old explained that rectangles and squares form "bottoms" of things like buildings, while triangles may form "tops," like a roof. She could imagine possibilities beyond and beneath the surface. This homework assignment is a tiny example, involving a tiny kindergartner in her first days of school, but it will happen again and again. This emphasis on the surface will miss the opportunity for something deeper. It is imagination's role to take us beneath the surface.

It is easy to see how natural imagination and play are for children. A stick becomes a sword; some cloth and stuffing becomes our precious baby; we become a passing bird. Our play and imagination become the means to try on new roles, comfort ourselves, and venture into the unknown. Imagination can serve as a laboratory of the mind where we can play out endless possibility. For our littlest friends, and perhaps our most creative, an imagined world is often the means to figure out how the world works, invent new possibilities, and give us hope. Picasso's way of bringing his unique perception and play to art and Martin Luther King's imagining a world of justice and equality—"I have a dream"—emerge out of their aesthetic and moral imaginations and take us beyond convention.

Imagination is typically understood as a kind of self-generated fantasy or idea and defined as "the act or power of forming a mental image of something not present to the senses."[2] Of course this is a powerful capacity, but one that has not often been encouraged in contemporary schooling or recognized for its value in domains very far outside of childhood or the arts. Imagination has often been dismissed as irrelevant or as a distraction from the educational enterprise ("Pay attention; you're daydreaming again") in favor of more "rational" or "real" concerns.

In general, there has been a tendency in the modern West not to take imagination seriously. The nonobservable, nonlogical nature of imagination renders it difficult to pin down and thus awkward in a rationalist, materialist backdrop. Imagination has been mistaken as merely a colorful accent to life, and largely dismissed in an educational age anxious about meeting standards and status. Imagination seems like the province of the child, the artist, or the daydreamer but not really appropriate for the serious learner. With respect to education, the dominance of developmental thought attempts to subsume imagination under our cognitive powers. In this view it becomes an aid to symbolizing, which is regarded as a transitional stage in a child's development and as such is cast as a mental activity not particularly necessary in later life.[3]

However, we do not outgrow imagination individually or culturally, as this process is fundamental to our knowing at every level of development. We hear, for example, that imagination is the source of insight, from scientific discovery to artistic innovation. The activities of mind that produced the inventions of da Vinci, the sonnets of Shakespeare, and declarations of liberty are not adequately explained through the mechanisms of sequential logic or sensory observation; some other process of mind is at work.

It is probably not much of a stretch to recognize some value in children's imagination and play or in the way that artists or fiction writers think, but when we look a little further we discover that imagination has been central for discovery and problem solving even in places like the hard sciences. Einstein framed the utility of the process in this way: "To raise new questions, new possibilities, to regard old problems from a new angle, requires creative imagination and marks real advance in science."[4]

Although we often assume science to proceed in very linear, rational steps, Polanyi's study of the process of *great* scientists describes the interaction of their knowledge and logic with something quite different.[5] We discover that the scientist's "quest is guided throughout by feelings of a deepening coherence. . . . We may recognize here the powers of dynamic intuition."[6] As Einstein tells us, "There is no logical path to these laws [of the cosmos]; only intuition, resting on sympathetic understanding of experience, can reach them."[7] Ideas and insights come as pictures or senses consistent with an imaginative process. For Einstein, breakthroughs emerged "as clear images which can be 'voluntarily' reproduced or combined."[8] Nobel Prize–winning physicist Eugene Wigner said, "The discovery of the laws of nature requires first and foremost intuition, conceiving of pictures and a great many subconscious processes. The use and also the confirmation of these laws is another matter."[9] These scientists, and plenty more, describe an imaginative and intuitive capacity of knowing that complements a more rational process.

Einstein is sometimes held up as the model of rational thought—logical-mathematical intelligence, as Howard Gardner put it [10]—but his thought process was characterized not only by logic and calculation but instead especially by imagination. He pictured himself riding on a light beam: "What will happen once I reach the speed of light?" While this requires logic to anticipate possible outcomes, it was an act centered on imagination that led to his radical insights. Einstein's work was essentially conducted as "thought experiments" in the laboratory of his mind. He considered this way of knowing so significant that he declared: "Imagination is more important than knowledge."[11] What he demonstrates so well is an integrative knowing: his knowledge of mathematics and physics held alongside his imaginative flights of mind enabled his stunning insights.

Jonas Salk, most famous for his invention of the polio vaccine, certainly had extensive knowledge, but it was a particular process of imagination, something he even had his own name for—"inverted perspective"—that he described as the key to unlocking insight.

> I do not remember exactly at what point I began to apply this way of examining my experience, but very early in my life I would imagine myself in the position of the object in which I was interested. Later, when I became a scientist, I would picture myself as a virus, or a cancer cell, for example, and try to sense what it would be like to be either. I would also imagine myself as the immune system and I would try to reconstruct what I would do as an immune system engaged in combating a virus or cancer cell.[12]

Through the insights gained he would then design laboratory experiments.

I would then know what questions to ask next. . . . When I observed phenomena in the laboratory that I did not understand, I would also ask questions as if interrogating myself: "Why would I do that if I were a virus or a cancer cell, or the immune system?" Before long, this internal dialogue became second nature to me. [13]

When I started to ask larger questions about the human world, it came naturally to me to play the same kind of game. . . . I sought a perspective from outside myself and outside the "here and now," as well as from within. . . . I have discovered that I can shift perspective from what I called the "here and now," to what I have named outer-time and outer-space. In doing this I was able to see relationships and processes that I had not previously seen. . . . I was able to imagine myself outside these phenomenon as well as inside them.

When I had had the experience of seeing from many different points of view, I could see and feel so much more; I then discovered what the words identification and empathy meant. [14]

He concluded, "I could manage to solve problems more easily because I could look at the problem from the viewpoint of subject and object at one and the same time." [15]

As it did for Einstein and Salk, King and Picasso, imagination builds a bridge between the known and the unknown. It enables us to ponder, play with, and generate new possibilities—to go beyond the information given, beyond the facts and the maps—in order to create new ways of seeing the world and create new worlds themselves. Few human capacities may be more important for our thriving and surviving. Nothing distinguishes the human mind any more than our capacity to imagine.

The integrative mind uses imagination on the one hand and knowledge or experience on the other. Einstein was able to use that ride on a light beam with his knowledge to uncover a new understanding of the world. Our imagination grounds us in the real tasks available around us. Great fiction writers invent their characters in a way that brings them to life, makes them believable, and even "real," we could say, as when the story captures something true about human nature and experience. Picasso said it this way, "Art is a lie that makes us realize the truth." [16]

The balance of experience on the one hand and imagination on the other is what empowers imagination in the world. Sometimes a fantasy can get us stuck in another world, becoming a delusion and ultimately keeping us from having much of a life outside that fantasy. However, as cosmologist Carl Sagan said, "Imagination will often carry us to worlds that never were. But without it, we go nowhere." [17]

BELIEVING BEFORE SEEING

Seeing before believing is the credo of modern science. We are encouraged to believe something only after we see it for ourselves. For the most part, this works just fine, providing the kind of verification that helps us avoid foolishness and superstition. However, it is sometimes necessary to believe *before* we can see. More precisely, this means suspending *disbelief* or a fixed view in order to open ourselves to some new possibility. Suspending disbelief does not mean abandoning critical reason or being a naïve convert to some belief or doctrine; rather, it means turning off our fixed perspective in order to see new possibility, the hope of something different.

One of our primary concerns as educators is to help students (and sometimes ourselves) find motivation. We know when someone is deeply motivated they will make remarkably dedicated effort to accomplish their goal whether climbing that mountain or graduating with the degree. While some students find intrinsic motivation in learning and others have a strong achievement orientation, it is not hard to find those who are apathetic and passive in the face of learning at every level. Apathy is often at the root of these learning failures, and apathy can often be explained by a sense of learned helplessness.

Learned helplessness essentially means that we believe we are stuck, without control and therefore unable to effect any change in our situation. We come to believe that we are powerless in relation to a task ("I can't do math") or perhaps more generally ("I'm not smart"), or maybe just that schooling seems meaningless or the world unfair or unyielding to our efforts. The result of this sense of helplessness in humans (and in nonhuman animals) is that even when there are options or ways out of our situation, we do not act on them or even recognize them. We remain stuck. Our imagination seems to have shut down.

As he entered high school, Hugh was a troubled and troubling underachiever. He was on the fast track to a disappointing life. Much to their frustration and worry, his parents and his teachers could not seem to nudge his apathy a bit. But his school had an unusual experiment at the time that involved periodically busing Hugh and a group of his peers to the nearby Princeton University campus where students listened to presentations by distinguished scientists of the day, Einstein among them. The hope was that these wise, or at least smart, men might have a positive impact on the lives of these difficult teens. Being in their presence might somehow rub off on them and magically straighten them out.

One day after a particularly long, dry talk by one of the physicists, a young girl sitting in the back of the tiered lecture hall raised her hand and wryly asked these men of science what they thought of ghosts. Her question was entirely off topic but after some chuckles around the room, the physicists took it on. The first fellow stood up and with an air of absolute certainty entirely dismissed any possibility of their existence. When he was done, the second scientist stood up to take his turn at her question. With great authority he rejected any chance whatsoever of ghosts, citing a lack of any hard scientific evidence. When they had finished, the third member of the group stood up. It was Robert Oppenheimer, head of the Manhattan Project, which had developed the first atomic bomb, and, once he realized what he had created, the staunchest opponent to its use (of course his protest was to no avail, as Fat Man and Little Boy were dropped over Nagasaki and Hiroshima, respectively, in 1945).

Oppenheimer, standing before the group of teens and a few peers, paused for a moment, and then said in response to the question about ghosts: "That's a fascinating question. I accept the possibility of all things." Given what he had seen already in his life we can suppose this was a statement borne out of first-hand experience. He went on to explain that "it is necessary to find one's own required evidence before accepting or rejecting a possibility."

For Hugh, hearing this response as he sat in this Princeton lecture hall was a moment of revelation that forever changed his life. Instead of closing down and accepting the world as prepackaged, which was the impression that he had received from schooling, Oppenheimer's perspective opened it back up to mystery, to the possibility of all things, and to one's responsibility to discover the truth for oneself. This gave Hugh permission for two things. The first was the openness to infinite possibility that comes from what poet W. B. Yeats called "radical innocence"—that moment of suspending disbelief and opening ourselves.[18] And simultaneously, there was the necessity and responsibility to find out for oneself, to be true to one's own standards rather than simply swallowing someone else's truth.

Hugh's inner life transformed as he came to define himself from the center of his own direct experience. He reported that he began to see the vitality and mystery of life, and to rely on his own standards rather than conforming to what others said was real or true or right or wrong. He dialogued with truth and took on the responsibility to determine it for himself. Life became about discovery, adventure, and invention instead of simply accumulating information that was "certain" or true and ultimately foreclosing of new possibility. Hugh Gunnison went on to become a distinguished, innovative, and irreverent professor who helped open up possibilities for others (me included, as he was my first graduate school professor). This moment helped him to believe in the possibility of all things—to believe so that he could see. He rediscovered imagination and with it a world of possibility.[19]

One way he translated his revelation into his own pedagogy was something I came to learn one day when I walked warily into his office early in a first semester of graduate school. I was sharing some half-baked idea and instead of correcting me, or saying "Yes, but . . ." he seemed to listen deeply and really try to understand what I meant. He asked probing but not attacking questions, reflected back his understanding, and in time, shared some of his own ideas, not in a correction but in a genuine and mutual dialogue. I began to see my ideas in a new, less defensive way; even more significantly, I saw myself differently. Being heard, validated, and then engaged in genuine dialogue popped something open in me. All those years of trying to conform to someone else's "right answer" or way of thinking had been internalized into a very loud self-critic; a voice that drowned out my own knowing to the point I did not trust or listen to myself very well. Previously, most of my schooling had been drudgery. It had such little life in it and seemed to have little to do with my life. After this conversation, my motivation exploded; something was freed up inside and the world opened up outside.

Performance

We learn from great performers, whether athletes, musicians, or others who have created remarkable success in their life that they often believe before they can see or do. That is, they often suspend reality and pretend.

Like many great performers, Greg Louganis, winner of five gold medals in Olympic diving, trained his muscles and his movements with discipline and commitment. But he also trained his mind. As part of his practice he would close his eyes, get relaxed and still, then imagine himself walking toward the pool, climbing up the ladder and out onto the diving platform. He would take a deep breath and then imagine himself pushing off into the air, feeling every rotation and the pull of gravity, seeing the perfect line of his body as it broke the plane of the water, feeling the impact on the top of his head or the bottom of his feet, tasting the water, hearing the crowd cheer as he came up for air, and feeling the deep satisfaction of perfection. [20]

Positive mental rehearsal, whether directed toward a flute performance or a math test, trains the mind to serve our goal. Imagination does not replace studying or practice, but it can take performance from mediocrity to mastery and help us get out of our own way.

This power of imagination has been used to help improve other kinds of performance as well. In a variety of studies, stroke victims who were left with impairment of their arm were given mental practice along with their standard physical therapy. After brief relaxation, patients were asked to imagine a task of daily living, for example, that their affected arm was reaching for, grasping, and lifting a cup to their mouth. Upon conclusion of the practice (depending on the particular study, from two or three times a week for six to ten weeks), blind measurement of these folks showed significantly improved function over those who only had the therapy or the therapy and a placebo activity. fMRI results taken before and after one study in particular also showed changes in brain activation in parts of the brain corresponding to improved arm functioning.[21]

We could imagine a variety of uses of this application of imagination, from test or other performance preparation to imagining ourselves in the scene of a history lesson. The bottom line is that suspending our disbelief and imagining new possibilities can help our imaginations come true.

THE DEMONIC

Diversity is the motor behind evolution, creation, and adaptation. It is difference, mutation, uniqueness that provides the pool out of which we crawl forward into new creative possibilities both as individuals and as a species. In many respects, reducing diversity therefore works directly against this natural process. Yet education is generally geared not toward diversity but most often toward something else. We find a system characterized by bureaucracy and standardization, from curriculum to testing. The risk of overemphasis on things that tend to provide the same perspectives in similar ways is simply that they limit diversity.

There are benefits of this way of shaping the world: standardized airport landing protocols, computer interfaces, and rules of the road allow us to function efficiently and safely, for example. We need common language and common understanding around many basic concepts in order to work together very well. It is reasonable to expect plenty of shared concepts and capacities in educational policy. But in the realm of living things, diversity engenders creativity. Entrepreneurial capitalism, for example, has been successful on the local and global stage not because it is the most moral, fair, healthy, easiest, or even most efficient, but because more than any other approach, it engenders creative diversity and thus invites innovation.

Culturally we are in an era of wrestling with the tension of homogenization, consolidation, and globalization in everything from farming to chain stores to mainstream media to medicine. We are weighing economies of scale and standardization that offer potential cost or control advantages against the loss of local ownership and responsiveness, independence, and diversity.

Homogenization, at its best, tends toward a degree of efficiency and control, and this has real and important value in many applications, but it is not the highest value for everything or all the time. It is an incomplete goal that has sometimes been mistaken as the end goal. When homogeneity overwhelms diversity, whether in a classroom or a culture, the available intellectual and imaginative gene pool starts to dry up. When it comes to human consciousness and creativity, unique ways of seeing and being catalyze growth and innovation. Of course in education we are speaking of a balance, but the domination of life and learning by the force of standardization, categorization, bureaucracy, and technology has such inertia that it is becoming increasingly difficult to find that balance.

One of the dangers is that the more complete, convenient, and comprehensive we assume a system is in meeting our needs or in describing reality, the more we will come to rely on the standards and processes of that system. The better the map or mechanism, the more we lean on it. The simulacrum becomes mistaken for what is real, the map for the territory. This is not an argument against maps or the value of educational architecture, it is instead a caution in the seductive power in such systems; to be seduced means that we have given over our responsibility to meet, create, and evaluate reality for ourselves. On the part of a teacher, imagination is surrendered to the convenience of the curriculum content, outcome, statistics, the computer program, management strategies, and more.

In the quest for living a life that matters, theologian Paul Tillich said there exists unusually powerful forces that can thwart and even destroy us. He had a name for this kind of power, one that captures just how dangerous it can be. He named these forces *demonic*. He did not use the term in the mythological sense of the devil or little demons running about, but instead as recognition that our creative nature can be overwhelmed by something else. The demonic is a force that is stronger than the individual's will, a force capable of overpowering our creative nature.[22] Addiction is an example of an individual's incapacity to resist possession by a drug. The influence of the Third Reich to turn scientists and schoolteachers into components in a genocidal machine is an example of how a force can overcome individual good will. Today, there is a mixed blessing in the ability to standardize, homogenize, and globalize. Both great good and great harm are possible when forces are so powerful and universal. The greatest threat is its potential to distort or estrange us from our authentic, creative nature without us even realizing it. When forces are so pervasive, we can hardly step outside their gravitational pull long enough to even recognize their influence on us.

De Tocqueville's dire warning about society in general speaks to education as well:

> It covers the surface of society with a network of small complicated rules, minute and uniform, through which the most original minds and the most energetic characters cannot penetrate. . . . It does not tyrannize but it compresses, enervates, extinguishes, and stupefies a people, till each nation is reduced to nothing better than a flock of timid and industrious animals, of which the government is the shepherd.[23]

Schooling's bias has been toward one right answer, toward a tyranny of truncated truth. This lends to easier assessment but not to a more adaptive mind or society. There is a story that makes the point for another goal. Sir

Ernest Rutherford, recipient of the Nobel Prize in physics, is said to have related the following story:

Some time ago I received a request from a colleague. He was about to give a student a zero for his answer to a physics question, while the student claimed a perfect score. The instructor and the student agreed to an impartial arbiter, and I was selected. I read the examination question: "Show how it is possible to determine the height of a tall building with the aid of a barometer."

The student had answered: "Take the barometer to the top of the building, attach a long rope to it, lower it to the street, and then bring it up, measuring the length of the rope. The length of the rope is the height of the building." The student really had a strong case for full credit since he had really answered the question completely and correctly! On the other hand, if full credit was given, it could well contribute to a high grade in his physics course and certify competence in physics, but the answer did not confirm this. I suggested that the student have another try. I gave the student six minutes to answer the question with the warning that the answer should show some knowledge of physics. At the end of five minutes, he hadn't written anything. I asked if he wished to give up, but he said he had many answers to this problem; he was just thinking of the best one. I excused myself for interrupting him and asked him to please go on. In the next minute, he dashed off his answer, which read, "Take the barometer to the top of the building and lean over the edge of the roof. Drop the barometer, timing its fall with a stopwatch. Then, using the formula $x=0.5*a*t^2$, calculate the height of the building."

At this point, I asked my colleague if he would give up. He conceded, and gave the student almost full credit. While leaving my colleague's office, I recalled that the student had said that he had other answers to the problem, so I asked him what they were. "Well," said the student, "there are many ways of getting the height of a tall building with the aid of a barometer. For example, you could take the barometer out on a sunny day and measure the height of the barometer, the length of its shadow, and the length of the shadow of the building, and by the use of simple proportion, determine the height of the building." "Fine," I said, "and others?" "Yes," said the student, "there is a very basic measurement method you will like. In this method, you take the barometer and begin to walk up the stairs. As you climb the stairs, you mark off the length of the barometer along the wall. You then count the number of marks, and this will give you the height of the building in barometer units. A very direct method. . . . If you want a more sophisticated method, you can tie the barometer to the end of a string, swing it as a pendulum, and determine the value of g [gravity] at the street level and at the top of the building. From the difference between the two values of g, the height of the building, in principle, can be calculated. . . . On this same tack, you could take the barometer to the top of the building, attach a long rope to it, lower it to just above the street, and then swing it as a pendulum. You could then calculate the height of the building by the period of the precession. . . . Finally," he concluded, "there are many other ways of solving the problem. Probably the best," he said, "is to take the barometer to the basement and knock on the superintendent's door. When the superintendent answers, you speak to him as follows: "Mr. Superintendent, here is a fine barometer. If you will tell me the height of the building, I will give you this barometer."

At this point, I asked the student if he really did not know the conventional answer to this question. He admitted that he did, but said that he was fed up with high school and college instructors trying to teach him how to think.

The student was Niels Bohr, Nobel Prize–winning Danish physicist and an innovator in quantum theory.[24] Although this is an embellished or even fictional account, the story makes the point nonetheless. Our challenge in educating is to engender creativity and not merely compliance, helping to keep imagination alive.

DIVERGENCE AND CONVERGENCE

Okay, ready or not, here is a test: Write down as many different uses you can think of for a brick.[25] What did you come up with? When we name a handful of conventional uses—building a house, a walkway, a fireplace, and not much more—we are using our memory but not much imagination. Our thinking converges on the familiar. When we play with the question a little differently we might think of a brick as a weapon, as a musical instrument, as a step to help us reach the top shelf or under the legs of our bed to raise it up, as a stop to keep the car from rolling back or the door from swinging closed. The ones with holes might be part of a water feature as liquid flows through those three small holes; maybe we could put a seed in each of the holes and fill them with soil. We could bring a brick to a basketball game to taunt the opposing team. Here is another test: Make up a story about 35,412.

It turns out that the questions like these were part of an initiative funded in part from a most unlikely source. The College Board, which prepares the oh-so-influential SAT, funded Professor Robert Sternberg's exploration to improve the test. The SAT test was designed as a predictor of who is likely to succeed in college. It has a reasonable degree of correlation but is in no way definitively predictive even though it is sometimes used in that way. But Sternberg found quite a different approach to predicting college success, and this included captioning cartoons and making up stories like those above.[26]

Sternberg's model suggests that success in college and in life is understood and predicted better by three interactive kinds of intelligence: analytic, practical, and creative. The analytic measures the familiar verbal, quantitative, and figural skills. The practical skills section might involve a story or video of a problem and then ask test takers to rate six proposed solutions from very good to very bad. Cartoons, making up stories, and the like are, as you would guess, about the creative. Sternberg's approach may indeed turn out to be a better predictor of performance in school, and in life, than the SAT. But more important than *predicting* one's success is developing the capacities to *improve* our chances of success, to grow our mind; cultivating imagination may help to do just that.

The capacity for divergent thinking is part of what makes up imagination's ability for supposition, flexibility, and inventiveness. Schooling is in the habit of working toward the "right answer," usually as quickly as we can. But our premature convergence on a solution can shortchange our understanding and the quality of our conclusions. Divergent thinking is an internal capacity that involves spontaneously generating ideas, from wonderful to wild to wacky. Coming up with as many possible uses for a brick or a blanket is an attempt to activate this divergent thinking.

Psychologist J. P. Guilford, who coined the concept of divergent thinking in the 1950s, saw it as a component of creativity and associated it with four main characteristics.[27] These were *fluency*—the ability to quickly generate a large number of ideas or solutions; *flexibility*—the capacity to consider a variety of approaches to a problem simultaneously; *originality*—producing ideas different from those of most other people; and *elaboration*—the ability to think through the details of an idea and carry it out.

We can also readily assume that certain attitudes support divergence and imagination. Both courage and playfulness help us overcome fear of being judged as wrong, foolish, or just different from the crowd. Likewise, an attitude of curiosity, which engenders pondering and puzzling with problems and gets us wondering what else we might see beyond the obvious, can help draw us into the adventure. It is easy to imagine how this is either invited or closed off by the culture of a classroom. Is it safe to experiment, to make mistakes, to bring forth wild ideas? Does the climate invite investigation, questioning, more than one answer or approach? Is the student rewarded or punished for imaginative thinking? Is there time taken for divergence? Are the ground rules for divergence clear and enforced (e.g., There is no judgment or criticism of ideas during divergent exercises)?

There are simple practices that help to enhance divergent capability. Whether in a group or working alone, *brainstorming* invites us to generate as many possibilities about a question or an issue without editing or judging their value or practicality. This idea generation, done alone or in a group, is a kind of adventure in thinking; we are just not sure where it will lead us. The key is to keep the ideas coming without any editing or evaluating whatsoever so that a free, spontaneous flow of consciousness is invited individually and as a group. A bit further into the process we might evaluate the relevance or practicality of an idea to pursue and then test out feasibility, perhaps converging on a best next step. But creativity often involves first and repeatedly the capacity to diverge from the given, the assumed, and our habits of mind in order to see in some fresh way.

Mind mapping is another simple tool to help generate and see new connections through representing ideas in a visual way—a map. In solving a problem, finding the right topic for a paper, or deciding on a career, simply write down a main idea or theme near the center of the paper. Then write down any related or even unrelated ideas that come up where you think they belong on the paper. You can draw lines of connections between various ones, use colored pencils, place various shapes around the words, draw the words in appropriate sizes, move them around, and so forth. See how their relationship changes over time as you return to the map. The idea is to represent these ideas visually and spatially and see if some connections, patterns, or something else begins to emerge into awareness. You may make a follow-up map deleting, adding, reshaping, and consolidating ideas further. This may provide a chance to see the issues nonlinearly. You may continue with drawings or at some point decide a particular organizational structure or theme emerges. This may then require a convergence of thought to corral the idea into a workable paper or outline, for example, or some other product or plan.

Free writing can also help activate our diverse, spontaneous imagination. Free writing involves simply taking a short time to write, unedited, as much as possible on a selected topic. For example, "Write about your life's work." The idea is to write down whatever comes to mind in a short period of time without editing or proofreading or any concern whatsoever for things like spelling or grammar. We might then take a few minutes to read what we just wrote, and follow that up with another five minutes of writing about what catches us by surprise or as important from the previous free write. If you need to get something done in a limited amount of time, spend five minutes writing and then five focusing and cleaning it up, another five writing and another five focusing. The process of generating and flowing with ideas is cognitively different than that of editing. Trying to combine these in the same stroke of the pen or keyboard can interfere with our progress. We just do not seem to make much headway despite a lot of strain. Peter Elbow's process approach to writing helps free up writer's flow and thus imagination in this way.[28] In each exercise the goal is a shift in consciousness from linear, categorical, realistic thought to free flowing, nonlinear, imaginative idea generation.

While divergent thought allows us to generate new possibilities, think in unusual ways, and imagine anything and everything, its cognitive partner is convergence. Convergence brings material from a variety of perspectives or sources to bear on a problem. It seeks an answer and can be used naturally to evaluate those divergent possibilities: "What is the best solution here?" "How can I determine which solution is best?" In problem solving it might clarify what the actual problem is: "What are we really going for here?" It might reflect on whether this is the question we really want to ask or whether there is another, more salient problem to solve. Convergent thought helps evaluate various options. Think of Jonas Salk designing experiments to test his imaginative hunches. Convergence, as it did with Einstein, could help us make a calculation, or use our knowledge of physics or behavior to evaluate which approach might work best. If divergence opens up possibilities, exposing the assumptions behind an issue, stepping outside its context and so forth, convergence pulls it back together toward a renewed understanding, a new structure or solution.

Convergent and divergent thought swings back and forth sometimes in an instant, at other times as different phases in problem solving. For example, we might have a concrete experience, form a question or a problem to solve, generate possible solutions, form a theory or hypothesis about such things, select a plausible solution, design an experiment to test the solution, and observe the results, bringing us back to concrete experience.

The problem is that our current emphasis is so geared toward answer and end product that divergence and diversity are often seen as a messy distraction rather than an opportunity for depth. So the argument is for raising the value of the messy, overflowing, nonlinear side of this partnership in order to open up new possibilities.

Thinking Tools

There are plenty of other ways to spark imaginative thought and grow the integrative mind. Like mind mapping or free writing, the approaches below are catalysts for knowing that serve as imaginative, cognitive, or thinking tools[29] in that their application can expand the process of knowing. These can be part of a teacher's repertoire available in any moment and adaptable for most any age group to invite an imaginative turn.

- *Difference*—such as inviting students to notice difference in degree versus differences in kind. "What makes this different (better; more or less beautiful, valuable, desirable, etc.) from that?" "How has this changed?"
- *Extremes*—help stretch our range of consideration: "What's the coldest thing you can think of?"
- *Metaphor,* (seeing one thing in terms of another; e.g., "Her hope was a fragile seed"), *analogy* (e.g., "He is like a rock"), and *simile* (e.g., "busy as a bee")—combine and connect ideas in endless ways and even leap conceptual levels: "That coldest thing you thought of, is it colder than the stare of an enemy?"
- *Symbols* (a flag, a cross, the flight of birds, superman, mother, a mountain)—represent rich patterns both uniquely individual and universal or archetypal. Thinking symbolically helps consider meaning that is more than meets the eye. "What does that flag (mountain, mother, etc.) evoke in you?" Recognizing recurrent human themes and characters in plays, histo-

ry, families, and society help students notice common patterns in the life around and within them.

- *Radical, silly, or "dangerous"* ideas—help challenge and play with conventional ideas and consider unconventional ways of seeing: "Tell a story about when you were president." "Fewer children should go to college." "We should implant memory chips in our brains."
- *Humor*—allows us to play with ideas and shake loose our conceptual frame. Sharing an emotional experience like laughter also helps to build a sense of community.
- *Wishful thinking, magic, or fantasy*—provides a kind of free ticket or open-ended possibility to bringing our own interests and desires into view. It helps activate emotion and relevance. "What would you do if you had a magic wand, a million dollars, . . .?"
- *Random entry*—Edward de Bono's thinking tool invites us to choose an object, sound, picture, or other stimulus at random, perhaps a noun randomly selected from a dictionary, and then associate it with the topic at hand.[30] Using the uninhibited style of brainstorming, the task is to make whatever associations and allow any new trailheads or connections to emerge.
- *Challenge*—a challenge tool simply invites the thinker to ask about the topic at hand in a nonthreatening way, why something or some process exists as it does.[31] Nothing is sacred or off limits; the goal is to challenge the existence or belief of anything in order to free up new possibilities. For example, "Why do we do things that way?"
- *Irony* and *sarcasm*—these tools begin to flourish for many in preadolescence, reflecting emerging cognitive capability. Helping students recognize and articulate irony helps sharpen thinking.
- *Storytelling*—at any age, creating a *story,* whether individually or as a group, provides a means to both create and learn to articulate a scene, integrating senses, emotion, empathy, logical progression, and more to bring depth and richness. Unlike a list, which also has its value, a story organizes understanding in a narrative that makes it easier to relate to and remember; stories can take on a life of their own as the flow of ideas gain momentum and find their own direction.
- *Myths*—these are typically fanciful stories that explain how or why things have come into being, for example: the origin of a people, the natural world, a society's ideals or customs. Both hearing and creating myths is a way to play with and exercise imaginative explanations.
- *Synesthetic* perceptions—taking up the merged or multiple senses of the body in unconventional ways expands experience from normative categories to dynamic perceptions: "What shape does that sound have?" "Do those words have colors?"

- *Pondering*—rather than focusing only on answers, inviting questions, especially open-ended questions, allows the imaginative mind to stretch beyond a narrow path. "What would you do if you were in so–and-so's shoes?" Collective pondering: "I wonder what it is like to be a terrorist . . . or a particular celebrity . . . or . . ." Physicist David Bohm explains that pondering and questioning "is not an end in itself, nor is its main purpose to give rise to answers. Rather, what is essential here is the whole flowing movement of life, which can be harmonious only when there is ceaseless questioning."[32]
- *Thought experiments*—allow for a reasoned and imaginative evaluation, inviting us to think through and evaluate the details of carrying out an idea. "What would happen if I did this?" "What would the world be like if the earth had no moon?"
- *Nature*—provides wonder for the mind. Its beauty and vitality stimulate the mind in ways we do not fully understand. Richard Lewis speaks of the way imagination and nature work together. "As children our playing brought us closer to these elements simply by our desire to touch what was there in front of us—and through our playing to imagine what it would be like to be a flower, a bird, a passing cloud, or the sweeping wind."[33] We could also consider other sources of profound stimulation, such as great art or even suffering.
- *Opposites*—often help us understand the thing we are looking at.[34] Whether in a first-grade classroom or for a doctoral dissertation, recognizing and articulating the opposite of something helps us to see the thing we are trying to understand more clearly as we see it in contrast. "What is the opposite of . . . ?"
- *Paradox*—The dynamic tension of holding opposing views simultaneously may produce a shift in our normal waking state, catalyzing the development of new schemata and opening to intuitive insight or synthesis. Jungian analyst Robert Johnson recognizes this shift in this way, "Conflict to paradox to revelation: this is the divine progression."[35] We might ponder the conflicting issues of fairness involved in a contemporary issue like affirmative action. Could we take both the position of the disadvantaged youth as well as the privileged child who was denied admission to college despite his or her higher performance? The point is not to win an argument as in a debate; it is to see beyond the various sides in order to take in the whole of the issue and synthesize a larger perspective. Holding contradictions serves as activation. As author Morris Berman writes, "The mind is moved to unfold itself in the space between contradictions."[36]
- *Dialectics*—in the nineteenth century, German philosopher Hegel devised an approach called dialectics, which became formulated into a simple process that involves thesis, antithesis, and synthesis. The *thesis* is an intellectual proposition. The *antithesis* is simply the negation of the thesis,

a reaction to the proposition. The *synthesis* solves the conflict between the thesis and antithesis by reconciling their common truths and forming a new proposition. Importantly Hegel said that a key purpose of dialectics is "to demonstrate the finitude of the partial categories of understanding."[37] By recognizing that any singular view is inevitably partial, we may remain flexible and open to new possibilities and more integrative views.

REAL IMAGINATION: *MUNDUS IMAGINALIS*

Just how central is imagination? While imagination is often described as a function of the mind, James Hillman suggests that rather than the mind being primary, it is imagination that is so.[38] Rather than an operation of the mind, the mind is a fantasy of the imagination. We do not need to resolve this in our own minds (or imaginations) but it makes the point that our presuppositions about our nature are, well, imagined.

Imagination is usually conceived of as an individual, subjective, idiosyncratic experience. Our daydreamed fantasy or creative image is thought of as generated from our own mind. But there is another understanding of imagination. The Islamic scholar Henry Corbin spoke of imagination not only as a kind of personal fiction but also as an objective and universal realm, what he referred to as *imaginal*.[39]

This *mundus imaginalis* is not a world of individual fantasy but instead a universal world considered more real than our daily physical existence. When we strive to bring some deep expression into form we are trying to capture that other realm and bring it into this one. A great piece of art or heroic tale may capture universal, archetypal themes or images that seem to resonate with us in some deep way—the hero's journey, for example, as Joseph Campbell popularized. The story of Romeo and Juliet or various similar tales represent ancient and enduring themes repeated over and over, from the Greek theater to Hollywood. The universal myths and symbols across cultures are signs pointing toward this other shared world. In some moments we recognize something that both expands us and brings us toward some sense of the familiar, toward what is universal.

In this way imagination may be considered more than a chance to exercise our creative muscles. It may also be a bridge to connect with the currents of our worlds. Imagination may attempt to explicate the implicate order, in physicist David Bohm's words.[40] The explicate is that which we can see and observe, the physical structure of the human heart, the trunk of that tree, and so forth. The implicate is the underlying pattern or energy that we cannot quite touch. In this sense imagination does not create image or art out of nothing; it reaches in to perceive something of this implicate order and then interpret and reveal it; it lifts a veil.

Evelyn Underhill, who studied the lives of famous mystics, understood such knowing in this way: The artist "by means of veils and symbols . . . must interpret his free vision, his glimpse of the burning bush, to other men. He is the mediator between his brethren and the divine, for art is the link between appearance and reality."[41] For Underhill, this is the power behind great art, heroic story, and mystic revelation in that it presents a faint image of this deep current. In this line of thinking, one's ability to recognize and represent that other realm relates to what we call genius. Underhill describes the underlying process of great art in this way:

> This intuition of the Real lying at the root of the visible world and sustaining its life . . . *must* be present if these arts are to justify themselves as heightening forms of experience. . . . That "life enhancing" power which has been recognized as the supreme quality of good painting, has its origin in this contact of the artistic mind with the archetypal—or . . . the transcendental—world: the underlying verity of things.[42]

Emanuel Swedenborg, an eighteenth-century Swedish scientist, philosopher, and theologian who wrote volumes on everything from metallurgy to marriage, also wrote about the ancient metaphysical law of correspondence. He understood that all things are basically stepped down manifestations of deeper realms. And when we reach and capture a glint of the universal in some way, Swedenborg implied that we grow soul.

In this view, the imaginal world serves as an intermediary realm that joins the transcendental or archetypal with the terrestrial one. Imagination builds a bridge between these worlds and carries us between them, thus serving as path and vehicle to integrate worlds.

As if testament to this way of considering imagination, Swedenborg's explorations in biology earned him credit for the first accurate explanations for the function of the cerebral cortex. He rejected the Newtonian concept of permanent, irreducible particles of matter and suggested that everything material was essentially motion arranged in geometric forms, *three centuries before* the understanding of molecules and DNA.[43]

Whether we think of this other world in terms of physics (Bohm's implicate and explicate order) or metaphysics (Swedenborg's correspondence or the archetypal) or simply seen and unseen, the point is that there is more than meets the eye and that the imaginative mind may have freer access, not being confined to the observable or rational.

There is always more to say, but I will end with two contemporary phenomena that take some imagination: Harry Potter and the commencement speech. These two converged one spring day in Harvard Yard. J. K. Rowling, author of the *Harry Potter* series, gave the 2008 Harvard commencement address, which she entitled, "The Fringe Benefits of Failure, and the Importance of Imagination."

Imagination is not only the uniquely human capacity to envision that which is not, and therefore the fount of all invention and innovation. In its arguably most transformative and revelatory capacity, it is the power that enables us to empathise with humans whose experiences we have never shared. . . . Unlike any other creature on this planet, humans can learn and understand, without having experienced. They can think themselves into other people's minds, imagine themselves into other people's places.[44]

Perhaps the most important aspect of the imaginative mind in education today is not directly about the student at all. Instead it is for the educator to imagine a greater possibility than the status quo, moving beyond the bureaucratic and the routine to find freshness, spontaneity, playfulness, wonder, joy, healing, and pure possibility. This is what we first imagined the life of teaching and learning to be: a sacred task that called to us then and now calls us again.

There has been a tendency in education not to take imagination seriously. However, imagination is fundamental to knowing at every level of development, across every significant domain, from scientific discovery to artistic innovation to practical problem solving. Additionally, imagination can provide a profound source of hope, vision, and therefore motivation. Diversity and divergent thought are central to imagination. A wide variety of specific thinking tools are readily available as catalysts in education at every level. However, contemporary forces of homogenization and standardization can work against diversity and thus pose a threat to the imaginative mind. Imagination may be understood not only as our individually generated image but also as a bridge between the known and the unknown, the visible and the invisible.

NOTES

1. Archibald MacLeish, *A Little Treasury of Modern Poetry*, 3rd ed., ed. Oscar Williams (New York: Charles Scribner, 1970), 887.

2. *Webster's New Collegiate Dictionary*, 11th ed., s.v. "imagination."

3. Edward S. Casey, *Imagining: A Phenomenological Study* (Bloomington, IN: Indiana University Press, 2000).

4. Albert Einstein and Leopold Infeld, *The Evolution of Physics* (Cambridge, UK: University Press, 1938), 92.

5. Michael Polanyi, *Personal Knowledge: Towards a Post-Critical Philosophy* (Chicago: University Press, 1958).

6. Marjorie Grene, ed., *Toward a Unity of Knowledge*, Psychological Issues Monograph, vol. 6, monograph no. 22 (New York: International Universities Press, 1969), 60.

7. Albert Einstein, "Principles of Research," in *Ideas and Opinions* (New York: Three Rivers Press, 1954), 226.

8. Albert Einstein, "Letter to Jacques Hadamard," in *The Creative Process,* ed. Brewster Ghiselin (Berkeley: University of California Press, 1952), 32.

9. As cited in Grene, *Toward a Unity of Knowledge,* 45.

10. Howard Gardner, *Frames of Mind: The Theory of Multiple Intelligences* (New York Basic Books, 2011).

11. George Sylvester Viereck, "What Life Means to Einstein: An Interview by George Sylvester Viereck," *Saturday Evening Post*, October 26, 1929.

12. Jonas Salk, *Anatomy of Reality: Merging of Intuition and Reason* (New York: Columbia University Press, 1983), 7.

13. Ibid.

14. Ibid., 10.

15. Ibid.

16. Pablo Picasso, "Picasso Speaks: A Statement by the Artist," *The Arts*, May 1923, 315–329. Later published in Alfred H. Barr, Jr., "Picasso: Fifty Years of His Art," exhibition catalog (New York: Museum of Modern Art, 1946).

17. Carl Sagan, *Cosmos* (New York: Ballantine, 1984), 2; original work published 1980.

18. William Butler Yeats, "A Prayer for My Daughter," line 66; *The Collected Poems of W. B. Yeats*, ed. Richard J. Finneran (New York: Collier Books, 1983), 189.

19. This account was published previously in Tobin Hart, *The Four Virtues: Presence, Heart, Wisdom, Creation* (Hillsboro, OR: Beyond Words, 2014).

20. Steven Ungerleider, *Mental Training for Peak Performance: Top Athletes Reveal the Mind Exercises They Use to Excel*, rev. ed. (New York: Rodale Press, 2005); original work published 1996.

21. S. J. Page, J. P. Szaflarski, J. C. Eliassen, H. Pan, and S. C. Cramer, "Cortical Plasticity Following Motor Skill Learning During Mental Practice in Stroke," *Neurorehabilitation and Neural Repair* 23, no. 4 (2009): 382–388.

22. Paul Tillich, *Systematic Theology*, vol. 1 (Chicago: University Press, 1951).

23. Alexis de Tocqueville, *Democracy in America*, vol. II (New York: Vintage Classics, 1990), 319; original work published 1835.

24. The barometer story was popularized by Alexander Calandra in his article, "Angels on a Pin," *Saturday Review*, December 1968.

25. Liam Hudson, *Contrary Imaginations: A Psychological Study of the English Schoolboy* (Harmondsworth, UK: Penguin, 1967).

26. Malcolm Gladwell, *Outliers: The Story of Success* (New York: Little, Brown and Co., 2008).

27. Joy P. Guilford, *The Nature of Human Intelligence* (New York: McGraw-Hill, 1967).

28. Peter Elbow, *Writing with Power: Techniques for Mastering the Writing Process* (New York: Oxford University Press, 1981).

29. For more on the concept of cognitive tools see, for example, Lev S. Vygotsky, *Mind in Society: The Development of Higher Psychological Processes,* eds. Michael Cole, Vera John-Steiner, Sylvia Scribner, and Ellen Souberman (Cambridge: Harvard University Press). See also Kieran Egan, *The Educated Mind* (Chicago: Chicago University Press, 1997).

30. Edward de Bono, *Lateral Thinking: Creativity Step by Step* (New York: Harper Colophon, 1990).

31. Ibid.

32. David Bohm, "Insight, Knowledge, Science, and Human Values," in *Toward the Recovery of Wholeness*, ed. Douglas Sloan (New York: Teachers College Press, 1981), 25.

33. Richard Lewis, "Our First Conversations," in *Only the Sacred: Transforming Education in the Twenty-First Century*, ed. Peggy Whalen-Levitt (Whitsett, NC: Center for Imagination, Education, and the Natural World), 4.

34. George Kelly, *The Psychology of Personal Constructs* (New York: W. W. Norton, 1955).

35. Robert A. Johnson, *Owning Your Own Shadow: Understanding the Dark Side of the Psyche* (San Francisco: HarperCollins, 1991), 9.

36. Morris Berman, *Wandering God: A Study in Nomadic Spirituality* (Albany: State University of New York Press, 2000), 8.

37. Georg Wilhelm Friedrich Hegel, *The Logic of Hegel: Translated from the Encyclopaedia of Philosophical Sciences*, 2nd ed., trans. William Wallace (Oxford: University Press, 1904), 149; original work published 1873.

38. James Hillman, *Archetypal Psychology: A Brief Account* (Dallas, TX: Spring Publications, 1988).

39. Henry Corbin, "Mundus Imaginalis or the Imaginary and the Imaginal," *Spring* (1972): 1–19.

40. David Bohm, "Insight, Knowledge, Science, and Human Values," in *Toward the Recovery of Wholeness*, ed. Douglas Sloan (New York: Teachers College Press, 1981), 8–30.

41. Evelyn Underhill, *Mysticism: A Study in the Nature and Development of Man's Spiritual Consciousness* (New York: E. P. Dutton, 1961), 75; original work published 1911.

42. Ibid., 74.

43. Ernst Benz, *Emanuel Swedenborg: Visionary Savant in the Age of Reason,* trans. Nicholas Goodrick-Clarke (West Chester, PA: Swedenborg Foundation, 2002).

44. J. K. Rowling, "The Fringe Benefits of Failure, and the Importance of Imagination," *Harvard Magazine*, June 5, 2008, http://harvardmagazine.com/commencement/the-fringe-benefits-failure-the-importance-imagination.

Final Words

At present . . . we are in that phase of transition that must be described as the groping phase. We are like a musician who faintly hears a melody deep within the mind, but not clearly enough to play it through. [1]

—Thomas Berry

To be a match for the reality of today and tomorrow a recalibration of mind is needed. Consciousness and culture have been thrown out of balance by the neglect of key ways of meeting and seeing the world. Like Berry's musician we can sense that something more is calling to us; we just have not quite been able to capture enough of the melody.

We do not need less reason or information or skills; instead we need more depth. We need a big enough inner world to be a match for the world in front of us, a more integrative way of knowing to understand more deeply the demands of our life.

The cultural change is already afoot. A more integrative, complex, holistic, interconnected worldview is already established intellectually at the leading edge of field after field, however little or much sway it actually has in corporate, political, or educational affairs at any given moment. However, these days require not only emphasis on worldview—as determined, defined, and definite, but especially on *world presence*: a dynamic, living process focusing on knower and knowing, not only knowledge. It is just this living balance of worldview and world presence that plays out in deep learning, allowing us to meet the world in a way that expands both knowledge and love.

These days require minds that are as uniquely imaginative as they are practical, as logically astute as they are intuitively sensitive, as able to see forest as they are tree, as attuned to information as they are to relations, as critical and calculating as they are available for awe and compassion. This

integrative mind represents the front edge of human consciousness and culture; and it becomes increasingly evident that it is essential if we are to thrive
and survive. The question is: How can education be part of this upgrade, a
catalyst for growing our humanity and thus society?

With a simple but subtle turn, our capacity for presence and nondefensive
openness, for balance and resilience, and for both witnessing and shifting our
mind grows from the inside out. This *contemplative* knowing provides the
inner technology essential to be a match for the external technology that is
shaping our minds and our daily life.

A more intimate empiricism, one sufficient to balance the detachment of
objectivity, enables us to enter the world. We come to participate rather than
dominate, meet rather than objectify. When we see the world through another's eyes we find both understanding and compassion rising to the surface, returning the heart to learning. This *empathic* mind opens communication, community, and communion with the world around us.

The most profound experiences and greatest motivations are most often
described as *beautiful*. Beauty somehow resonates deep within us, showing
us glimpses of both immanence and transcendence all at once, yet it has been
neglected in schooling. Nature, as the most enduring source of beauty, provides inspiration, awe, and wonder for the mind.

A more *embodied* knowing bridges the abstract and concrete as we bring
hand, heart, head, and gut back together to their natural unity. The body and
mind are not associated or connected but unified in a whole system, providing a robust way of knowing.

Imagination allows us to reach beyond the given and explore endless
possibilities. This is the fuel for creation and creativity, essential for problem
solving, taking us beyond the status quo and overcoming the compression of
homogenization, bureaucracy, and the like.

At this moment in history, we are being called to a new level of understanding: called by the gaps between the haves and the have-nots; called by
the unprecedented possibility and peril that exist today; called by the knowledge that fixation on test scores or standardized curriculum or technology has
not grown our humanity nor seems likely too; and called by the fact that our
most significant experiences of reality are not consistent with our educational
enterprise. The solution at the edge of this new episteme is not so much about
what we know but especially about how we know. As Thomas Berry said,
our opportunity is to move from seeing the world as a collection of objects to
experiencing it as a communion of subjects. In so doing we grow our humanity, the ultimate sustainable goal for education and society.

NOTE

1. Thomas Berry, *Dream of the Earth* (San Francisco: Sierra Club Books, 1990), 47.